"Our deepest disappointment is not living true
from both western psychology and mindfulness
shines a clear light on our habits of seeking approval, and offers meditations that free us to live from our own natural compassion and intelligence."

—**Tara Brach, PhD,** author of *Radical Acceptance and True Refuge*

"*The Need to Please* is an important book. It reveals the pain of leaving yourself and looking for love in all the wrong places. You will discover that all you've been longing for is within you—that it was never outside of you. May this wise book with its practices of mindfulness and compassion guide you into your heart."

—**Bob Stahl, PhD,** coauthor of *A Mindfulness-Based Stress Reduction Workbook*, *Living with Your Heart Wide Open*, and *Calming the Rush of Panic*

"This impressive book describes how the practice of mindfulness can bring new awareness to moments of acquiescence that are driven by fear, self-doubt, or rejection. Written with kindness and sensitivity, it provides an experientially grounded road map for recovering elements of true worth and inner strength that can inform a more authentic approach to interpersonal encounters."

—**Zindel V. Segal,** author of *The Mindful Way through Depression* and professor of psychology at the University of Toronto

"With clarity and skill, Micki Fine's book deepens understanding by illuminating the root causes of the struggle and anxiety associated with needing to please, and step-by-step, engages the reader in a path of discovery and freedom through the practice of mindfulness and kindness."

—**Florence Meleo-Meyer, MS, MA,** director at the Oasis Institute for Professional Training and Education at the Center for Mindfulness, University of Massachusetts Medical School

"This wonderful and practical book will help you release your dependence on others' approval and find the self-acceptance and kindness you actually need."

—**Kristin Neff,** author of *Self-Compassion*

"*The Need to Please* is a step-by-step guide that shows how to progress at your own pace, toward your own specific goals, in ways that are most comfortable and useful to you. Readers will develop a deeper love for themselves and others, as well as a more peaceful and fulfilled life experience. Give it a try—you won't be disappointed!"

—**Linda Bell, PhD,** professor of communication and family health, Indiana University, and a mindfulness-based family systems therapist and supervisor

"The beautiful book is truly precious for all of us who have been caught in the trance of unworthiness and felt that we needed to become pleasing in order to be loved or even tolerable. Fine offers us a way to dispel this trance and discover peace, love, and happiness in our lives just as we are."

—**Steve Flowers, MFT,** author of *The Mindful Path through Shyness* and coauthor of *Living with Your Heart Wide Open*

"Why *The Need to Please?* Because we assume life begins someplace other than where we are right now. And we've swallowed the notion that we, in this moment, are not enough. Fine gives us the permission to pause and be mindful and gentle with ourselves and embrace the ordinary and extraordinary riches—beauty, compassion, generosity, creativity, and meaning—inside each one us. It's a gift to read. It's a gift to give."

—**Terry Hershey,** author of *The Power of Pause* and *Soul Gardening*

The Need to Please

Mindfulness Skills to Gain Freedom from People Pleasing & Approval Seeking

Micki Fine, MEd, LPC

New Harbinger Publications, Inc.

Publisher's Note

Distributed in Canada by Raincoast Books

New Harbinger Publications, Inc.
5674 Shattuck Avenue
Oakland, CA 94609
www.newharbinger.com

Cover design by Sara Christian; Text design by Michele Waters-Kermes;
Acquired by Jess O'Brien; Edited by Jasmine Star

Library of Congress Cataloging-in-Publication Data

Fine, Micki.
The need to please : mindfulness skills to gain freedom from people pleasing and approval seeking / Micki Fine ; [foreword by] Diana Winston.
pages cm
Summary: "In The Need to Please, a leading mindfulness expert and psychotherapist provides compassionate, mindfulness-based techniques that will help chronic people-pleasers address and overcome their fears of failure, inappropriate self-sacrificing, loss of personal identity, and voracious need of approval"-- Provided by publisher.
Includes bibliographical references.
ISBN 978-1-60882-608-7 (pbk.) -- ISBN 978-1-60882-609-4 (pdf e-book) -- ISBN 978-1-60882-610-0 (epub) 1. Self-perception. 2. Interpersonal relations. 3. Mindfulness-based cognitive therapy. I. Title.
BF697.5.S43F56 2013
158.2--dc23

2013024303

Printed in the United States of America

15 14 13
10 9 8 7 6 5 4 3 2 1 First printing

To John Thomas Pavlicek,
dearest husband and love of my life

Contents

Foreword

In my twenties, I found myself at a crossroads. I had been a good girl for most of my life: I ended up at a prestigious college; I excelled at being a dutiful daughter and student; I volunteered in my spare time, tirelessly taking care of others and working for social change. I had done everything right.

But underlying it all was a profound sense of unhappiness. In my mind, I was never good enough, no matter how much praise I received, no matter how hard I tried to be perfect, agreeable, and helpful. I plagued myself with criticism, aiming for perfection and always falling short.

My turning point was the incredible good fortune to stumble on mindfulness teachings while traveling abroad in India. I saw how through compassionate, moment-to-moment awareness, I could attend to my experience and not be so overwhelmed by it. I was fascinated by the insights into my mind and the relief I began to feel from self-judgment. I plunged myself wholeheartedly into mindfulness.

Over many years of practicing both in daily life and in retreat in the United States and Asia, I found that something fundamental began to shift.

Through mindfulness I worked with self-criticism, mindfully vigilant for the voice that told me I wasn't good enough or that my worth was dependent on others. Every time these judgments arose, I noticed, softened, and ultimately began to see through them. This awareness, in combination with a good dosage of practices that cultivate positive emotions—especially self-directed kindness and compassion—created a whole new inner landscape, one of much more care and self-acceptance.

It didn't happen overnight, and it wasn't necessarily easy. But without a doubt, it worked. Twenty-five years later, I can see the vestiges of these habits, but they're mostly shadows at this point.

I am certainly not the only person who has struggled with these issues, and in my current role as a mindfulness teacher, I have encountered thousands of students who have been crippled by similar issues. In fact, so pervasive is this tendency that I sometimes refer to it as an epidemic, one that affects countless people of all ages and genders and from all backgrounds.

How I wish Micki Fine's book had been available twenty-five years ago. It probably would have saved me and many others a lot of struggle.

Nonetheless, in 2013 I'm immensely grateful for this amazing book. It is just the right antidote to the epidemic of self-hating and people pleasing.

This book takes readers by the hand, lovingly and nonjudgmentally walking us through the whys and hows of chronic people pleasing. Micki's compassionate and expansive approach invites us to try it ourselves. Her thoughtful analysis explains the mechanisms behind chronic people pleasing, interweaving her expertise in both mindfulness and psychology to show us how all aspects of our lives can be touched by this affliction—and ultimately healed.

Micki is a skilled guide into this territory because she has a deep and long-standing personal practice, from which she draws much of her understanding. This personal experience perfectly complements her skill as a therapist. Micki knows this material from the inside out. She shares her own personal journey of healing through mindfulness and loving-kindness practices, and she also shares stories of clients with whom she has worked over the years. Her beautifully structured explanations, stories, exercises, and practices can help all of us heal from the shame and blame of self-hatred.

These practices work. They really do. I have watched countless students try these practices, just as Micki has laid them out, and over time I have seen these students find their way to more love and self-compassion. And Micki furthers the work by adding many new psychological tools, practices, and perspectives.

This book is a gift to all of us. Delve in. Try it. Experiment. Be aware. Be kind. You have a wonderful guide in your hand. May it transform you!

—Diana Winston
Director of Mindfulness Education
Mindful Awareness Research Center
University of California, Los Angeles
Author of *Fully Present: The Science, Art, and Practice of Mindfulness*

Acknowledgments

I am in awe of the everyday kindness, support, and generosity that my husband, John Thomas Pavlicek, has demonstrated throughout our marriage. John has helped me know and experience love, acceptance, compassion, and creativity. His unwavering belief in me has helped me share mindfulness practice from the beginning of my career as a mindfulness teacher right through writing this book. I am forever grateful to John, the love of my life.

My admiration and love goes out to Ketria Bastian Scott, my friend and administrative manager. She brought beauty, creativity, and organization to the process of taking over various administrative duties so I could focus on this book. I deeply appreciate and trust her creative ideas, decision making, and follow-through in all matters. She is an angel straight from heaven.

I am deeply grateful to my life teachers and meditation teachers: my parents, Grant and Mercedes Webster; my sisters, Dana Webster, Kim Clement, and Robin Perko; and Sister Elena Shiners, Mary Meyerson,

Linda Bell, Susan Packwood, Bette Lenz, Diana Winston, Jon Kabat-Zinn, Thich Nhat Hanh, and Jack Kornfield.

I send great appreciation to those who read drafts and coached and supported me during the process of writing this book. In the early days, Charlie Scott provided valued coaching and helped me believe I could write this book. Bette Lenz, Ceil Price, Ketria Bastian Scott, Dana Webster, Trina Jones Stanfield, Kim Clement, Lucia McBee, Nancy Simpson, and Sue Young all contributed to reading and reflecting on the book. I love you all.

To editors Jess Beebe and Nicola Skidmore at New Harbinger, and copyeditor Jasmine Star—thank you for your clarity and guidance. And to Jess O'Brien and everyone else at New Harbinger, thanks for shepherding the book from beginning to end.

Introduction

There I was, ten years old, precariously perched on the highest bar of the swing set, my little hands gripping the big bar. My best friend, Teresa, convinced me that I could hold on to the bar just right, flip forward, swing myself all the way around, and come up sitting on top of the bar where I started. So I tried. I swung forward with all my little girl might—and plop. I landed flat on my back on the ground eight feet below.

You might say that little girls just do silly things, but let's take a deeper look. I took that plunge because I wanted to please my friend and make her love me. For years, I had been taught to look to others for what I should do and try my hardest to please them. I believed that if I didn't do that, they wouldn't love me and might leave. I was so well trained to please others that I flung myself in harm's way.

This training came from receiving inadequate demonstrations of love and acceptance, coupled with consistent, harsh criticism from many adults in my life. Though well-intentioned, they were unable to demonstrate their love for me exactly as I was. My heart was wounded, resulting in beliefs that I was unworthy of love and responsible for other people's happiness, and that I had to do everything possible to please them or risk being abandoned. This shaped my life and relationships for many years.

That incident at the swing set was just one of many in which I relinquished my own well-being, even my own safety, to make others love me. I spent a significant part of my life unconsciously struggling to please others so that I might be loved and they wouldn't leave me. Throughout my early life, I metaphorically flung myself from the swing set over and over again. I jumped when anyone said "Jump." I tried my hardest to be nice and accommodating. I said yes when I didn't want to. I tried to anticipate what others wanted from me. While many people thought I was Miss Congeniality, inside I felt increasingly anxious, resentful, and depressed.

In the midst of a life transition in my thirties, I found two amazing processes that helped me explore and open to my inner life: mindfulness and psychotherapy. Psychotherapy helped me explore my past and how it affected me in the present, and assisted me in learning positive ways to live, one being mindfulness. Mindfulness is the awareness that arises when we bring openhearted, nonjudgmental attention into the present moment. I sometimes jest that mindfulness saved my life, but there may be some truth to that statement. The practice of mindfulness helped me know love and freed me significantly from the suffering caused by my limiting beliefs.

Since you have this book in your hands, it may well be your time to explore mindfulness. This powerful practice has helped millions of people find peace and love in the midst of the challenges of life. If my story sounds at all familiar, I hope you'll read on and explore how mindfulness and the approach in this book can help you liberate yourself from a chronic need to please others.

The Organization of This Book

Because mindfulness is at the core of the approach in this book, chapter 1 explores the basics of mindfulness. This foundation will allow you to practice mindfulness while reading this book. Chapter 2 examines the common childhood wound that starts the cycle of chronic people pleasing.

Chapters 3 and 4 focus on chronic people pleasing and the related thoughts, feelings, behaviors, and relationship dynamics. In the process, you'll learn more about how this cycle, which is intended to help you gain love and acceptance, actually creates further disconnection from yourself and others. Rest assured that this work is not about becoming selfish. Pleasing others is a valuable part of life, and most religious and spiritual traditions teach that taking care of and loving others is one of the highest forms of spiritual practice. However, when pleasing others is motivated by feelings of unworthiness and fear of not being loved and perhaps even being abandoned, it becomes an unhealthy, compulsive, and painful cycle.

This cycle consists of deep feelings of unworthiness, excessive attempts to be or do what you think others want from you, worry about meeting those supposed demands, and sacrificing your own well-being to please or fit in with others (Braiker 2001). If you're caught in it, you'll say yes even when you don't want to, don a mask of chronic niceness, apologize for everything, and disconnect from your innate loveliness and ability to follow your own life path. Salman Rushdie described this cycle when he talked about being "sealed in a cell in which one experienced an interminable torment and from which there was no escape" (2012, 284).

However, there is a way out of this interminable torment: mindfulness. Chapters 5 through 12 will help you develop mindfulness and apply it to the cycle of chronic people pleasing. This can help you heal childhood wounds and nurtures qualities such as self-compassion, intentionality, and calm responsiveness—qualities often stifled by a lifetime of chronic people pleasing. This will allow you to release the fear that drives approval-seeking behaviors and open the door to loving others more authentically and wholeheartedly, finding greater balance in your relationships, and enjoying a fuller sense of appreciation for life.

Each chapter explores a topic and suggests ways in which you can practice what you've learned and take time to reflect on how it fits into your life. Throughout, you'll find experiential exercises to help you integrate what you've read. In addition, I offer various mindfulness meditation practices to help you make mindfulness part of your daily life. My website includes a page, www.livingmindfully.org/ntp.html, where you'll find resources related to this book, such as guided audio recordings in various lengths for many of the meditations in either MP3 or CD format.

The Road Map

The practical goal of this book, gaining freedom from chronic people pleasing and opening up to unconditional love, is a journey. When embarking on any sojourn, we need to know our point of departure, the means of travel, and the destination. Conscious awareness is essential to this journey and will allow you to understand and truly feel that freedom, ease, love, and joy are available to you in any given moment. The journey begins with mindfulness, which is also the means of travel and the destination.

You may have heard the saying that life is a journey, not a destination. This is key to the practice of mindfulness, and to liberating yourself from a cycle of chronic people pleasing. As you practice mindfulness, your experience will teach you that each moment of your life is the only moment in which you can learn and grow.

The Point of Departure

When we go exploring, we typically don't spend time thinking about our point of departure. However, knowing your starting point is essential if you are to get to where you want to go. For example, when making airline reservations, you have to specify your departure point in order to be routed successfully. To chart your journey toward genuine love and freedom from chronically seeking the approval of others, you need to become aware of the characteristics of your current habitual ways of feeling and thinking: feeling unworthy of love, frequently focusing on what others are thinking of you, taking a subservient position in relationships, and so on. Once you know where you are now, you can practice nonjudgmental awareness to help discern which of the painful experiences of chronic approval seeking are true for you.

The Method of Travel

Mindfulness is also the means of travel toward freedom from people pleasing and approval seeking. The practice of mindfulness can help you wake up to life as it is and recognize the moments in which you forsake yourself in order to please others and the times when you feel unworthy or afraid that others won't like or love you. Then, you can handle moments like these with the awareness and compassion that mindfulness breeds, rather than the denial, reactivity, and harshness you may have experienced in the past. I also suggest that you extend mindfulness to the thoughts, feelings, and judgments that come up as you read this book so you can simply experience the book and perhaps read it with a more open and compassionate mind.

The Destination

Of course, the destination is also important. As you work with this book and with mindfulness, you'll travel toward letting go of fear, opening to love, healing the wound that causes chronic people pleasing, boosting self-respect, creating balance in relationships, and freeing yourself to choose your own path in life. Mindfulness can help us accept life as it is, gain the freedom to say no when needed, face conflicts with loved ones and resolve them peaceably, and feel loving toward others instead of obliged to them.

At the outset, it's important to be clear about where this journey *isn't* going. When I say "freedom from chronic people pleasing," I don't mean ceasing to want to please others or never doing so. I don't mean taking care of only yourself or having a devil-may-care attitude toward other people and their needs.

Being free from chronic people pleasing and approval seeking actually includes caring deeply about others and their welfare as you open to your deep, internal capacity to love through mindfulness. Along the way, you'll find that you already have what you've been searching for through approval seeking. Your capacity to care for others out of love instead of fear will be enhanced as you no longer equate your significance and survival with taking care of others.

When you open to your nature of love and let go of fear, many things can happen. Attention that has been focused on others is freed to devote to whatever is most important in the moment. You can worry less about what others think of you. You can be more engaged in your own life and let yourself focus inwardly on your values to understand what adds meaning, purpose, and joy to your life. You can learn who you are, what is most deeply important to you, and how to take care of yourself.

Befriending yourself and your emotions will enhance your ability to be compassionately assertive and loving both with yourself and with others.

As you free yourself from chronic approval seeking through mindfulness, your relationships can become more loving, balanced, and connected. Through mindfulness practice, you can open to your innate love and compassion for yourself and others. This helps liberate you to love more freely, be open to your loved ones' concerns, and take care of both you and your loved ones in a fearless, loving way.

How to Use This Book

It's important to read with an open mind so you can connect with the ideas on the page. However, don't believe what is written until you reflect on it or, better yet, try it for yourself. Take a cue from Albert Einstein, who believed that the source of all knowledge is experience (2011). See for yourself and value your experience. This is important, especially if you've spent years looking to others for validation. Experiment with tuning in to your thoughts and feelings about what you read, and then decide if it's true and right for you.

In addition to explanatory text, in this book you'll find exercises, reflections, and meditations to help you engage in what you're reading about. When doing the exercises and reflections, I recommend that you practice a few minutes of meditation first, to help you settle in a bit. I'll provide instructions for a few meditation practices you can use in this way. Also, bear in mind that the exercises and reflections are intended to provide an opportunity for self-discovery. Because this is your unique journey, there isn't a single, perfect, right way to engage in them.

I encourage you to try all of the exercises and practices in this book, but to do so without pressuring or pushing yourself, as this would simply perpetuate the tendency to be harsh with yourself that comes with chronic people pleasing. Rather, experiment with being kind to yourself, letting go of judgment, and cultivating a sense of exploration.

Journaling

I recommend that you keep a journal to record your experiences with each exercise. After connecting with your breath, check in with the bodily sensations, thoughts, and feelings that arise as you engage in the exercise. Bring an attitude of open-mindedness, compassion, and non-judgment to your writing. Don't worry about the quality of the writing, just get your thoughts and feelings down as they come along. Consider writing, rather than typing, your journal, as the process of writing can help you slow down and carefully reflect on the topic.

My Intentions

While reading my descriptions of chronic people pleasing and approval seeking, notice the self-judgments you make and how you hear my voice as the writer. My intention for this book is to foster compassionate awareness of chronic people pleasing and welcome you to the practice of mindfulness, but never to blame or shame you. I hope that what you read encourages you to commit to practicing mindfulness for a few months so you can discover whether this practice is for you. You won't know unless you try.

1

Mindfulness

Grant sat feeding an early morning bottle to his newborn son, Will. The walls were tinted with the dawn's color, and Will was adorable. Grant considered moments like these precious and often found peace in them.

However, on that morning he was troubled, yet only vaguely aware that he was worrying. His wife, Abbie, had asked that they have a discussion, in *that* tone of voice. Grant was worried that he had upset her again and feared that she might leave him, taking the baby with her and making his worst nightmare come true. When he managed to notice his preoccupation, he felt tension in his body and irritation at himself for feeling apprehensive, and then told himself to get a grip. Soon enough, he grabbed his cell phone to contact a colleague, even though he was still feeding Will.

We all have times like these, doing one thing while the mind is off on a trip to the past, the future, or a daydream. We spend most of our lives mind tripping, not fully engaged in the life that's right in front of us, and some difficult things can happen as a result.

First, we miss out on what's important in the moment. Being preoccupied with what Abbie had said in the past and his fears about the future, Grant missed out on the feel of the baby in his arms, the tug on the bottle as Will sucked hungrily, the smell of Will's hair, the preciousness of his tiny hands, and his feelings of unconditional love for his son. By picking up the phone, he also avoided his emotions—and tried to avoid the whole situation. Unfortunately, this happens a lot. More often than not, we leave the present moment unattended, even though this is the only moment we genuinely have.

In addition, just like Grant, we typically aren't aware of what the mind is up to and how our unnoticed thoughts can lead us into difficulty. On Grant's future-oriented mind trip, he was living a moment that might not actually happen, at least not in the way he anticipated. Understandably, it left him feeling anxious and disconnected.

What kind of trips does your mind go on when you leave it unattended? Are there patterns of thought that keep you stuck in approval-seeking mode? Where is your attention most of the time? Is your mind focused on what others think, what you should do to please someone, or how you can fit in?

Another troublesome trait of the mind is attempting to suppress, banish, or get rid of difficult experiences and grasp for pleasant ones. Grant did this by pushing away his fear and desperate longing to be loved, chiding himself, judging his emotions, and then getting busy so he didn't have to notice his feelings. This is a completely natural reaction, but it actually exacerbates an already difficult situation.

Fortunately, there is an antidote to these problems: mindfulness. Mindfulness is the awareness that arises when you intentionally bring openhearted, nonjudgmental attention to the present moment. You can practice mindfulness with anything, from the world around you to your own thoughts, emotions, and physical sensations. With practice, you can choose to be present, opening the door to learning from difficult experiences, including when you feel hijacked by the need to please others.

In this chapter, I'll explore the practice of mindfulness and how it can help free you from the kinds of pitfalls that Grant experienced: not being present for meaningful moments of life, unconsciously taking mind trips to scary places, and struggling to avoid painful feelings, all of which can lead to suffering. Mindfulness practice can help you understand and relate to all of your experiences with less reactivity and more compassion.

This will enhance your ability to act wisely instead of reacting reflexively and afford you the freedom to change painful, chronic people-pleasing behaviors.

The Origins of Mindfulness

Mindfulness meditation has been practiced for over 2,600 years. It's based in Buddhist thought or, as some people describe it now, the science of the mind. (Don't worry; you don't have to be a Buddhist to practice mindfulness meditation.) In 1979, Jon Kabat-Zinn, PhD, and his colleagues started the Mindfulness-Based Stress Reduction (MBSR) Clinic to help patients at the University of Massachusetts Medical Center. This small beginning flowered into the world's largest stress-reduction clinic, hundreds of MBSR clinics, and thousands of peer-reviewed studies about the effects of mindfulness. If you're interested in more information about the research, www.mindfulnet.org is a good resource.

The Practice of Mindfulness

Mindfulness is the awareness that arises when we bring our attention into the moment and notice and let go of judgments, critical thoughts, and preconceived ideas. So often our attention is restricted to *thinking* about our experience, particularly how we think things should be and what we can or should do about it. With mindfulness, we more directly attend to the experience of our lives through our senses, rather than through automatic, reflexive thoughts that narrow our attention. This allows us to see the moment with more clarity and openheartedness.

Mindfulness is an innate human capacity, and anyone can cultivate it, including you. Young children show us how natural this capacity is. I experienced this with my goddaughter, Elizabeth, when she was just a toddler. While swinging backward on a swing, she noticed her barefoot toes and joyfully cried, "*Toes!*" Upon swinging forward, she looked up and exclaimed, "*Sky!*" Her fresh eyes gave her a sense of vibrancy, a sense of "Wow!" You too were born with this capability. Inside, you already have everything you need to practice mindfulness.

Two branches of practice—formal and informal—provide avenues to reconnecting with these qualities of aliveness, nonreactivity, openness, and compassion. *Formal practices* are characterized by setting aside time, apart from daily activities, to meditate. In this book, I'll teach you several formal practices. *Informal practice* involves intentionally cultivating present-moment, nonjudgmental awareness during your everyday experiences. For example, you can notice the warmth or coolness of your hands, the smell of coffee, or anxious or joyful thoughts and feelings. Formal and informal practices nourish one another, working together to build awareness, compassion, and steadiness.

Awareness of the breath is an integral part of both formal and informal mindfulness practices. Bringing attention to the breath anchors us in the body and our direct, sensate experience and is often the primary way we come into the present moment.

Informal Practice: Stopping to Take a Breath

Because the breath is such a helpful anchor for mindfulness, let's begin there.

Right now, stop briefly and come into the moment by taking a conscious breath. Notice various sensations associated with the breath: the coolness of the air as it enters and the warmth of the exhaled air, your abdomen or rib cage gently expanding and contracting, or the sound of your breath or the way it feels in your nose or mouth. Just tune in to whatever you notice about your breath without trying to change it in any way.

You can do this brief informal practice anytime, anywhere. Attending to the breath in this way can help you feel steadier, even during difficult times when you feel compelled to please others. For example, when someone expresses an opinion with which you disagree, stopping to take a breath and come into the moment provides you with a bit of time before you respond. This can give you more freedom to forestall an automatic reaction, such as nodding your agreement just to be nice.

Informal Practice: Eating Mindfully

Here is a common and classic mindful eating practice created by Jon Kabat-Zinn (1990). For this practice you'll need two raisins or another type of natural food, preferably a couple of small morsels.

Pretend that you've never seen these objects before. Look at them through new eyes, like Elizabeth did with her toes and the sky. Examine them with all of your senses, saving the sense of taste for last. What do you see? Perhaps you notice size, wrinkles, colors, or shape. How about your sense of touch? Do these morsels feel sticky, squishy, or malleable? What do you notice through your sense of smell? If your mind wanders away, gently bring it back to noticing the objects. Can you hear the objects? Perhaps they make a noise if you squish them between your fingers up close to your ear.

Notice what you experience in each moment, including the sensations in the body as you bring one of the morsels to your mouth. Hold it in your mouth for a while before you begin to chew. What happens in your mouth? Perhaps you notice a rush of saliva. Perhaps the object plumps up. When you begin to chew, take plenty of time. Notice the flavors, what happens in your mouth, the sensation of swallowing, and how the food feels going down your esophagus.

Next, eat the second object as if you've never eaten one before.

***

Welcome back. What did you notice about the raisins or other food? Most people have a much richer and fuller experience of the food than usual, and this helps them realize how much they're missing out on in life. Many people have a little "aha!" moment when they realize that the way they pay attention affects their experience, and that they can apply this to other aspects of life. Can you imagine how things might be different if you were to pay attention to other daily experiences, including emotions and thoughts, in this way?

Showing Up for Extraordinary Moments in Daily Life

Some people wonder why they should pay attention to seemingly mundane daily activities. But as you may have gathered from the raisin exercise, just because an activity occurs every day doesn't mean it must be ordinary. Because this moment is the only one we have, it makes sense to show up for it and experience it.

Moreover, when we're present in the moment, we can recognize more quickly when we go on a mind trip. That way, we won't travel so far from the moment. For example, if you're on an approval-seeking mind trip, you might anticipate what you could do to get someone's approval. If you're consciously aware of that thought, you may be less likely to spiral into worrying and then reacting with people-pleasing behaviors that don't serve you well. If you aren't aware of that thought, you're likely to react to it unconsciously and have little to no choice about how you behave. In addition, paying attention to daily activities can train your attention so that you can be present more often, even when facing challenges.

Informal Practice: Being Mindful During Daily Activities

To practice informal mindfulness of daily activities, choose a task, such as making your bed, brushing your teeth, washing the dishes, or simply sitting and working and attend to your experience of it. Commit to bringing the new eyes of mindfulness to the activity. For example, when washing your hands, feel the temperature of the water and the slipperiness of the soap. Smell the scent of the soap, and hear the sound of the water running and your hands rubbing against each other to create lather.

Informal Practice: Using Cues for Mindfulness

Choose something that happens throughout the day and make it a cue to stop, take a breath, and be present. Here are some examples:

- *Waiting for your computer to boot up or shut down*
- *Taking a sip of a beverage*
- *Standing up*
- *Sitting down*

Informal Practice: Using Your Smartphone Smartly

Program your smartphone or computer to provide a gentle reminder to take a breath and be present. There are several mindfulness apps that can assist you with this.

The Eyes of Kindness and Compassion

As you allow yourself to be present more often, you will become aware of both joyful and painful experiences. As this happens, a dose of compassion is in order. Mindfulness naturally opens you to the compassion that is already inside you. Awakening compassion toward yourself and others can help you see life through the eyes of kindness and mercy instead of harshness and loathing.

Aversion and Grasping

Compassion and steadiness of breath can be essential tools when you're caught in the grip of painful people-pleasing moments. Although suffering and difficulty are natural parts of life, it's instinctive to try to avoid them and grasp onto something better. We've acquired these survival techniques over millennia, and they serve us well. For example, if a bear runs at you, your avoidance instincts will ignite and drive you to fight or flee.

However, problems arise when avoidance and grasping extend to our inner life. We try to run from painful situations by diverting our attention from them or denying or suppressing our emotions about them. We try to hold on to or even enhance pleasant events, which may cause us to miss out on everything these moments have to offer. Have you ever felt angst when you thought of vacation ending, even though you still had several days of vacation left? Most of us have felt this way. The problem is, it impairs our ability to enjoy the days of vacation that remain.

Being trapped in a cycle of chronic approval seeking can be similar, as you deny anger about always catering to others and cling to being nice all the time so others will like you. But when you struggle in this way, you actually add to an already difficult situation. For example, by trying to get rid of anger, you may actually feel angry with yourself for feeling angry, creating more internal distress. This also robs you of the chance to resolve the underlying problem.

Through mindfulness, you can learn to stop running from whatever you encounter in the moment, turn toward your experience, and meet it with kindness. This helps you to see the moment more clearly and create more options for resolving difficulties. This attitude of allowing and accepting is not passive; it's a courageous stance of acknowledging and experiencing the truth of the moment so that you can more skillfully decide what needs to be done, if anything.

Alex, a twenty-five-year-old hospital administrator, came to me for mindfulness training to address feelings of anxiety and unworthiness she had run from most of her life. After being turned down for a promotion and receiving painful criticism from her boss, she was worn out from anxiety and the constant worry about what others thought of her. She said that her attempts to please weren't serving her well and that it was time to change.

As a child, Alex's parents wanted Alex to be safe and never suffer, so they solicitously hovered over her, making most decisions for her. Alex wasn't allowed to explore her way of living in the world and grew to doubt her opinions and needs. She tried to anticipate what others wanted of her and watched for signs of approval. She believed that this would win her love and approval. She also became highly critical of herself in nearly everything she did, especially when she made a mistake.

During our work together, she came to understand how she suppressed her emotions by tending to others' needs until she was exhausted. This left her with unfinished emotional business, and she noticed that her anxiety was followed by anxiety about feeling anxious, followed by criticism of herself for feeling that way. In the end, her attempts to avoid painful emotions only increased her feelings of anxiety, unworthiness, and irritability.

Alex displayed a lion's courage in addressing her feelings of anxiety and unworthiness. One day I invited her to kindly attend to the feeling of anxiety without trying to change or fix it. I asked her to close her eyes and let go of her struggle with the emotion by grounding her awareness in the bodily sensations of her anxiety. As I watched, a frown arose and then softened, tears came and went, and finally a distinct calm came over her body. When she opened her eyes with a smile on her face, she said that she wasn't afraid of herself anymore.

Of course, this wasn't the end of Alex's challenges. Some days she was able to befriend her experience, and other days she struggled and fought with it. But all in all, she felt more capable of handling her emotions with kindness. Several years later we met by chance, and she said that mindfulness practice was the best thing that she had ever done for herself.

Formal Practice: Mindfulness of the Breath

Understanding mindfulness comes more from the practice of it than from reading about it. So now let's practice a short mindfulness meditation. Ideally, you'd set aside about ten minutes for this practice, but you can adjust the time if you need to.

Find a private, comfortable place to sit where there are a minimum of distractions and potential interruptions. You can sit on a cushion on the floor or in a chair with your feet flat on the floor. Either way, sit so that you feel grounded, comfortable, alert, and dignified, embodying the qualities of awareness and ease you're cultivating.

You can close your eyes or keep them open; either is fine. If you keep your eyes open, find a place to gently maintain your gaze so your eyes won't help your mind wander too much.

> *Start by making a gentle intention to pay attention—to be awake and aware.*
>
> *Now, notice the whole body sitting...feeling the body being supported by the earth...*
>
> *When you're ready, notice the fact that you're breathing... Observe where you feel the breath most easily and let your attention settle there... It might be in the nostrils...the back of the throat...or the chest or belly... As best you can, bring awareness to the entire breath... following the physical sensations for the full inhalation, any pause, the full exhalation, and finally any pause before the next inhalation.*
>
> *Allow the body to breathe by itself...not controlling it in any way. Bring an attitude of allowance to the whole experience of the meditation. You don't need to make anything happen, especially relaxation. This meditation is about cultivating awareness. Relaxation may come as a by-product.*
>
> *Notice the wandering mind...and take no blame for it. The mind is simply going to wander, and it isn't your fault. So, briefly acknowledge the mind wandering and let go of any judgment or blame, then gently come back to the breath. Experiment with bringing a sense of kindness toward the wandering mind.*
>
> *You may find it helpful to label the thoughts with names, such as "daydreaming," "worrying," or "planning." Experiment with seeing the repeated wanderings of the mind as a way to cultivate patience and gentleness toward yourself.*
>
> *As this practice draws to an end, allow yourself some time to ease your attention back into the outside world by noticing what you see as you open your eyes (if they were closed), what you hear, and so on.*

***

Welcome back. What did you notice during the meditation? Do you have any concerns as a result of the meditation? I recommend that you explore the practice you just did so you can learn to meditate with greater ease. Take a few minutes to write about your experience in your journal.

Working Skillfully with Meditation

Here are some ideas that might be helpful as you begin to develop your meditation practice. Understanding these points will hopefully make it easier for you to continue to practice and to practice often.

Wandering Mind

Most people find that the mind wanders away from the breath repeatedly—sometimes within seconds of focusing on it. Just knowing that everyone's mind wanders can help you feel less distressed about it when it happens to you. In addition, understand that the mind wanders *all by itself*. In other words, you're not to blame for it.

Each time the mind wanders, simply acknowledge it, let go of any blame or judgment, and come back to the breath, again and again and again. To help steady the attention, some people find it useful to silently whisper to themselves, "in-breath," "out-breath," or both.

Noticing the wandering mind in this way can teach you many things, and we'll continue to explore this throughout the book. One thing it teaches is that you don't have to react to every thought or urge that arises. Over time, this will help you learn that you don't always have to leap to please others. More broadly, it will help you learn to let go of any struggle to make certain things happen. Instead, you can simply rest in the breath.

Expectations

Most people begin a mindfulness practice with expectations and goals, such as quieting the mind and feeling relaxed. The deep desire to feel better is healthy and natural. However, a focus on goals takes us out of the moment and can cause anxiety and a sense of dissatisfaction.

This also applies to goals we may have for meditation. When we're focused on a goal for meditation, we expect it to be a certain way. We try to *make* it happen, and we evaluate our progress toward the goal. Although these kinds of efforts may seem helpful in achieving a "good" meditation, they actually get in the way and cause us to lose track of the simple focus on present-moment experience. For example, if a meditation doesn't go the way we wish, we feel frustrated with what *is* happening in the moment and end up in a fight with ourselves. Attachment to the goal and aversion to an alternative experience leave us feeling frustrated and dissatisfied. As a result, we may increase our efforts to achieve a goal, causing even more misery, or we may give up altogether, depriving ourselves of the benefits of the meditation.

Reflection: Exploring Your Expectations

Reflecting upon what you've read can help you clarify your thoughts. Take some time now to explore any expectations or goals you have about meditation. You might have expectations of what mindfulness will do for you, how that will happen, or whether you'll see results. When you did the formal Mindfulness of the Breath exercise, what did you want to happen? Did you struggle to make anything happen while you practiced? Spend a few minutes writing about this in your journal. As outlined in the introduction, first take a moment to connect with your breath, then check in with the bodily sensations, thoughts, and feelings that arise as you think about these expectations. Don't worry about the quality of the writing, just get your thoughts and feelings down as they come along.

How to Handle Expectations

Some goals and expectations that people have for meditation are to control thoughts, quiet the mind, or relax. Trying to achieve these goals is a bit like expecting a two-year-old child who is throwing a tantrum to calm down by forcing her to be still. This usually results in the child becoming overstimulated and defiant. Similarly, in meditation, your mind will be more active if you try to control it, and your body won't relax if you try to force it. This makes it nearly impossible to feel calm and peaceful. Paradoxically, the best way to quiet the mind and relax is by not trying to achieve these states.

That's easier said than done, so here are some tips that might be helpful. Before you meditate, check in with yourself and acknowledge any expectations or desires. Gently encourage yourself to foster kindness, patience, and an attitude of just seeing what happens. In addition, remember that you're not to blame for the mind wandering, and that coming back to the breath again and again is as much a part of the meditation as staying with the breath. When you notice that the mind has wandered, in that very moment you are present again. So when you notice the mind wandering, let go of evaluating yourself, acknowledge yourself for being present again, and come back to the breath.

A related expectation that can turn mindfulness meditation into a struggle is expecting yourself to stay focused for the entire meditation. In doing so, not only do you leave the moment, you may feel as though the meditation is going to last forever. The suggestions above also apply to this expectation, along with this additional advice: Only expect yourself to pay attention to the current inhalation, and after that, only expect yourself to pay attention to the current exhalation. In other words, let go of expecting yourself to pay attention beyond the present moment. Having realistic expectations can help you deal with the reality of the wandering mind and give you the gift of resting deeply in the moment.

Chronic People-Pleasing Expectations

The guidance for dealing with expectations during meditation also applies to your expectations that you must please others. Experiencing how goals in meditation cause distress instead of peacefulness can help you see how the struggle to gain love and security at the cost of your well-being does the same thing. Shining the light of awareness on chronic people-pleasing goals and expectations by simply acknowledging them puts you on a pathway toward freedom from them.

For example, let's say that you've been asked to serve on a committee of an organization for which you volunteer. You might vaguely feel overextended already, but your normal, automatic response would be "Of course I will." With mindfulness practice, you can stop, take a breath, and acknowledge your expectation that you should please others no matter what. This may allow you a moment in which you can free yourself from your habitual reaction and instead respond consciously and skillfully.

Reflection:
Exploring Your Approval-Seeking Goals

Take a few minutes to practice mindfulness of the breath, and then reflect on what you've just read. What approval-seeking goals do you get caught up in? What happens when you focus excessively on achieving those goals? What feelings do you experience when you're caught up in evaluating your progress toward those goals? As recommended in the introduction, when journaling, bring an attitude of open-mindedness, self-compassion, and nonjudgment to yourself and your experience.

Attitudes to Bring to Mindfulness Practice

In *Full Catastrophe Living* (1990), Jon Kabat-Zinn wrote about certain attitudes to foster in your mindfulness practice, including patience, beginner's mind, nonjudging, letting go of striving, and allowing. Practicing mindfulness will cultivate these qualities, and practicing these qualities will cultivate mindfulness. I encourage you to commit to practicing , which I have adapted, with permission, from Kabat-Zinn's work, as often as you can in daily life.

Patience

Patience is essential for living a peaceful life and cultivating mindfulness. As Francis de Sales, bishop of Geneva in the fifteenth century, is reputed to have said, "What we need is a cup of understanding, a barrel of love, and an ocean of patience." More recently, Jon Kabat-Zinn wrote, "Mindfulness does not bulldoze through resistance. You have to work gently at the edges, a little here and a little there, keeping your vision alive in your heart, particularly during the times of greatest pain and difficulty" (1990, 299). Practicing patience can help us understand that most things arise through a process of unfolding. For example, a butterfly emerges from its cocoon slowly, and if you try to help it out, the butterfly will die. Along the same lines, if you try to force yourself to change immediately, you may feel frustrated and give up.

It can take some time to change entrenched, long-term habits of chronic people pleasing. You'll need to be patient with the process. Likewise, please be patient with yourself as you cultivate mindfulness. It's likely that no one ever taught you how to pay attention in this way. Since you have other habitual ways of paying attention (or not paying attention), you'll need to be gentle and patient with yourself as you work to unlearn these patterns. If you practice patience with your mindfulness practice and people-pleasing patterns, it's likely that you can stick with the process and develop greater trust in yourself and better balance in your relationships.

Beginner's Mind

Once, as I guided a seventy-year-old client through an awareness exercise, he experienced the extent to which he took things for granted. He sadly said, "I look but I don't see, and I listen but I don't hear." As he continued to reflect on this, a few moments later he blinked away tears after realizing that he hadn't been present that morning when he said good-bye to his wife.

For many reasons, we all take things for granted and forget to tune in to the richness of the present moment. With beginner's mind, we instead look at each moment, situation, and experience as if encountering it for the first time. To apply this to people pleasing, notice what happens inside when you're about to say "I'm sorry" for something that isn't your fault. By noticing the experience with beginner's mind, as you did with the raisins, you can offer yourself a fresh perspective that can lead to greater understanding.

Nonjudging

As you notice your thoughts more often, you'll probably notice how often you judge just about everything. Making judgments is a part of being human, and it often serves important functions. Unfortunately, the mind has taken this to excessive levels, constantly judging everything, which can leave us feeling discontented. And because these judgments are so automatic and unconscious, we tend to react automatically based on them, which adds to the problem.

For example, if you've been conditioned to think you have to earn love, you may see a friend doing something, immediately make the judgment that he needs help, and then jump in to assist him. However, this judgment may not be accurate. Your friend may have the situation under control and resent your intervention. If so, what started as a strategy to obtain approval backfires.

The practice of mindfulness can help you more clearly see judgment as judgment, an important step in reducing the tendency to judge and buy into your judgments. You may then be able to open to new responses instead of reacting based on judgmental thoughts.

Nonstriving

Daily life tends to be filled with getting things done and accomplishing goals. As a result, our attention often isn't in the moment. Of course, it's difficult to be satisfied and peaceful in the moment when we're focused on making things different than they already are. Instead, we may feel anxious and dissatisfied, which makes it difficult to act responsively and skillfully.

This is similar to hitting a tennis ball. If you get ahead of the moment and think about the ball flying back at your opponent instead of watching the ball, feeling your body, and using your muscles to skillfully hit the ball, you might miss it. Staying in the moment can help you make contact with the ball. Likewise, staying in the moment can help you make contact with life.

When you notice expectations in everyday life, recognize them as such and then experiment with adopting an attitude of "let's see what happens." This can help you be more open to whatever is happening in the moment instead of struggling to create a certain outcome.

This nonstriving attitude is important in the practice of mindfulness. If you use mindfulness to try to get rid of a feeling or an experience, such as frustration or the wandering mind, you'll probably only add to your struggle. Simply noticing the present moment with an open heart, again and again and again, without trying to make anything happen, is what fosters change.

Allowing

Cultivating patience, beginner's mind, nonjudgment, and nonstriving breeds the ability to allow the moment to be as it is, helping you see it more clearly. Likewise, allowing yourself to be exactly as you are will help you experience the acceptance you didn't receive enough of as a child. As a result, you can stop struggling to obtain this acceptance from others. Instead, you can rest in the moment and respond to life with less reactivity. You can extend this attitude of allowing to your meditation practice by accepting any mind wandering or restlessness that happens during a meditation.

Given how goal oriented our culture is, and how ingrained the belief that we must please others can be, it's a brave act to bring a stance of allowing into our lives. When we can be present to our experiences just as they are, we don't have to waste time and energy denying or resisting them or trying to force things to be different than they are. Through mindfulness, we nurture this attitude of allowing and, ultimately, freedom.

Sudden and Gradual Awakening

While there are immediate benefits to practicing mindfulness, its effects are also gradual and cumulative. As we practice being aware and open in the moment, over time our awareness and acceptance of the moment are refined and strengthened. We not only pay attention more often but "differently and more wisely—with the whole mind and heart, using the full resources of the body and its senses" (Williams et al. 2007, 55).

Knowing this can help you allow your practice to be as it is in the moment, with trust in its unfolding. For example, most people who are new to mindfulness describe immediate benefits such as feeling more alive and relaxed. With continued practice, people tend to experience other benefits, such as freedom from lifelong habits; this comes over time and also varies from day to day. I encourage you to allow your practice to evolve naturally without trying to force it to conform with any expectations you may develop based on the examples and stories in this book.

Exercise: Encourage Yourself to Practice Mindfulness

Take a few minutes to practice Mindfulness of the Breath. Then sit quietly and check in with your thoughts and feelings about mindfulness. You might be feeling that this book and the benefits of mindfulness will help you. You may have doubts about your ability to practice mindfulness or whether it can make a difference. Whatever is happening inside of you, acknowledge it, let go of any judgment, and encourage yourself to commit to experimenting wholeheartedly with the practice of mindfulness. You won't know if mindfulness is for you unless you try.

Summary

Having read this primer in mindfulness and tried a few practices, you may have more questions than when you started, particularly if you're new to mindfulness. Notice and let go of any struggle and hold your questions lightly, allowing them to raise your curiosity and fuel further exploration.

I encourage you to practice regularly and make your practice your own. Make a special point to listen to your heart and intuition when making decisions about your practice, especially since part of people pleasing is doing things in ways you think others would approve of. This book gives suggestions, not rules for your practice. I recommend that you start by trying what is suggested and see if it fits for you.

Mindfulness practice takes energy, time, courage, and commitment and asks you to look deeply into the moment, whether it's joyful or painful. As mentioned, mindfulness practice is not necessarily easy, but it is meaningful and worthwhile. Please remember that it is through the process of purely and simply paying attention with an open heart in the moment, again and again and again, that you can gain freedom from the need to please.

2

How People Pleasing Develops

Let's revisit Grant from chapter 1. As his day continued, Grant repeatedly found himself dreading the conflict with Abbie that he'd built up in his imagination. He was willing to do just about anything to make her love him and stick with the relationship, including walking on eggshells to keep the peace, which is exactly what he'd had to do with his father. As a child, Grant's father demanded that he strictly follow the rules, and if he didn't, he risked punishment and rejection. As he worried about Abbie, Grant's past was creeping into the present moment.

In this chapter I'll discuss the childhood wound that typically causes chronic people pleasing: not receiving unconditional love from our parents and caregivers. In addition, I'll explain how people pleasing arises as a natural response to this wound. This knowledge can help you see the past clearly and understand how it affects you in the present. It can also help you understand that the past isn't you, and it isn't your fault. This perspective can give rise to kind understanding, self-compassion, and the ability to let go of reactivity and allow the present moment to be less influenced by past injuries.

Unconditional Love

Feeling connected to and caring toward someone without wanting anything from that person is a hallmark of unconditional love. Revered in spiritual and psychological writings, not to mention countless popular songs, this kind of love is boundless, immeasurable, and freely given. It recognizes the person's inner loveliness and is independent from what the person thinks or feels or how she acts. Thus, love abides even when the beloved does something "wrong" because her true, radiant nature is seen as unmarred by the behavior. In other words, it is the beloved's behaviors that are considered problematic, not the beloved. With unconditional love, the beloved doesn't have to earn love; it is given freely.

In regard to children, this doesn't mean they should be allowed to act in any way they want, but that caregivers provide compassionate and age-appropriate discipline, direction, boundaries, and guidance. When children receive unconditional love from caregivers, they feel safe and are assured of their inner beauty. They form strong connections with their caregivers and reap a host of other benefits and blessings. Knowing at a very basic level that they are loved and worthy of that love helps them believe in their goodness and allows them to project that belief out into the world. They can open to their true nature of love, engaging in life fully, experiencing love, and extending love to others. This authentic connection is often considered to be the core of psychological well-being.

Feeling Unloved and Unlovable

The desire to be completely loved and accepted is hardwired into all of us. However, it is impossible to give or receive unconditional love consistently because all humans share a common wound from childhood, though the degree of that wound varies. At least occasionally, all children have experiences in which their inner beauty isn't reflected to them through their caregivers' consistent, loving acceptance of who they are (Welwood 2006). As a result, we are all somewhat cut off from an awareness of our innate, internal worthiness.

Another childhood dynamic contributes to feelings of unworthiness. As children, because our parents are bigger than we are and know more than we do, we believe that they're all-powerful and wise. This belief is important in helping us feel safe, and because we rely on our caregivers for survival, it isn't easily shaken. Therefore, we believe our caregivers even when they say or do things that are abusive, unloving, or unaccepting and then assume that we are innately flawed.

Then, to avoid being hurt again, we disconnect from our emotions and bodies, where we actually feel the sensations of love: warmth, expansiveness, ease, or tingling, to name a few. This numbing becomes the norm. In addition, because our original experience of love is receiving it from others, we believe that love originates outside of ourselves, and we look for proof of it from others (Welwood 2006). This further disconnects us from our own nature of love. Accordingly, we compulsively strive to earn love and are fearful of the possible consequence of not receiving it: abandonment.

Additionally, since our caregivers' support was essential to our very existence and the desire for unconditional love is deep, we adaptively tried to think our way into their good graces, giving rise to some of the thought patterns and emotions associated with chronic people pleasing (these thoughts and emotions are described in chapter 3). This sets us up for more pain and suffering as we try to obtain perfect love while at the same time being cut off from it.

Making things even more painful, approval-seeking behaviors by their very nature can never yield the experience of unconditional love. After all, they involve doing something in an effort to earn love.

You might think the desire for unconditional love is a problem. But the problem lies not with the desire itself, but in how we react to that desire: believing that if we try hard enough and become worthy, we can earn it. Another problem is that it simply isn't possible to receive consistent unconditional love. So although it isn't inherently problematic to long for this love, too often that desire is held up as a standard, and we end up thinking the love that *is* available from others isn't enough. As we try in vain to satisfy this unquenchable thirst, we often end up confirming the belief that we are unworthy and unlovable.

It isn't surprising that this childhood wound results in habitual people-pleasing behaviors and relationships that are fraught with problems. Fortunately, there is a solution: when we open to our innate, inner loveliness and our deep desire for love, we can heal the wounded heart and realize that we already have the love we need inside us. Mindfulness practice can bring this awareness. Through this deep opening, we can give love, sometimes even unconditionally, and accept and find joy in the love that we do receive, unconditional or not. We become less reliant upon others for proof of our worth because our hearts are more resilient and less wounded.

• *Madeline's Story*

Madeline, a fifty-year-old physician, came to me for mindfulness training at the recommendation of her therapist. Madeline felt despairing, depressed, unloved, and unlovable. Despite of being highly successful academically and in her career, for as long as she could remember, she'd felt there was something deeply wrong with her.

When Madeline was a child, she was subjected to abuse, neglect, and, tragically, the suicide of her mother. Madeline was told that her mother didn't want her, which contributed to Madeline's feelings of being deeply ashamed, unworthy of love, and responsible for her mother's death. These feelings went underground as Madeline cut herself off from love in spite of her desperate desire for it. After her mother's death, she was punished if she expressed her grief. She felt as if she had no choice but to restrict herself to doing whatever she thought would keep her safe and promote even a remote chance of receiving love and acceptance. Madeline absorbed herself in household chores and taking care of her siblings, leaving little time to tend to her emotions and needs for friendship and play. Whatever acceptance she did find was from her teachers. This gave her hope that things would be better once she got out on her own and got a good education.

As a young adult, she attempted to gain acceptance by excelling at school and work, but she never felt recognized for who she was, only for her accomplishments. It always seemed that she could never do enough to prove her worth. Because of her belief that she was unworthy and unlovable, she settled for a marriage that was unfulfilling and even abusive at times. Her children were the only joy in her life.

Through mindfulness and loving-kindness meditation (discussed in chapter 7), along with psychotherapy, Madeline gradually found freedom from her childhood wound. While on a meditation retreat, she was still and silent long enough to experience how she had been looking in vain for the unconditional love she wanted from her mother, and how she had judged all love that came her way as insufficient. In the stillness, she experienced the life-altering revelation that she had love inside herself that wasn't dependent on anyone. This insight was a direct effect of her willingness to be quiet, observe her experience, and purposefully cultivate the love that had been obscured by her childhood wound but was still inside her.

How We Experience Being Unloved

It isn't difficult to understand that, at any age, people would feel unloved and unlovable when subjected to abuse and neglect. But chronic people pleasing can develop even in children raised within loving, stable families. Situations that can set us up for a lifetime of people pleasing include receiving conditional love, not being valued for who we are, not getting a say in decisions that affect us, and, of course, abuse and neglect. The strength of the chronic people-pleasing cycle depends on the severity of the circumstances that created feelings of being unloved and unlovable.

Conditional Love

A subtle but prevalent reason for feeling unloved is caregivers doling out love based upon the child's compliance with their expectations and withdrawing it when the child doesn't live up to their standards. Of course, parents want children to do well in school and in life. But when signs of love are withdrawn because children don't live up to expectations, children learn that they aren't acceptable exactly as they are. When they make mistakes and are treated with disdain or criticism or simply ignored, they learn that they are not okay.

There are many ways in which love can be conditional, and, of course, parents differ in the way they withhold their love. Some parents may heap harsh, degrading judgments on their children and dole out serious and sometimes abusive consequences for even minor mistakes. Other parents simply withdraw displays of love when the child doesn't comply with their demands. Still others close themselves off from their children more subtly when they aren't compliant.

Not Being Valued for Who You Are

Sometimes parents see their child as an extension of themselves and try to mold him into their image, foisting their desires upon him. They fail to honor who the child is and whether their wishes are fitting for him. In their book *Everyday Blessings*, on mindful parenting, Myla and Jon Kabat-Zinn (1997) aptly describe a person's unique nature, personality, and life purpose as sovereignty. When a child's sovereignty is overlooked or disrespected, he concludes that who he is doesn't matter.

One of my mindfulness students, Brigid, a thirty-year-old graduate student, described herself as being an introverted child and her mother as a powerful, extroverted businesswoman. Brigid's mother often chided her for not being more outgoing and showed disdain for the introverted activities that Brigid preferred. She would tell Brigid to "get a backbone" on a regular basis. As a result, Brigid developed the belief that she wasn't okay the way she was and that something was inherently wrong with her. Instead of blossoming into her unique nature, she strove to be what her mother wanted and became anxious and depressed in the process. She worked in marketing and sales but found her job unfulfilling. As she opened to herself, she pursued becoming a yoga teacher and a psychotherapist. This work felt right for her, and as she moved in this direction she felt more grounded and in control of her life path. And as she established her own identity and became more confident, she also found ways to develop a loving relationship with her mother.

Not Getting a Say

Sometimes habitual people pleasing stems from a child's unconscious assumption that she doesn't know what's best for her because caregivers, teachers, or other key adults always made decisions for her. If children aren't encouraged to explore and learn from their own experience, or if their thoughts, opinions, and desires aren't valued, they don't learn to find their own way in the world and instead look outside themselves for guidance on what to do. In addition, they may develop the belief that they don't matter. Over time, their inner wisdom and unique nature are buried, and they lose touch with themselves.

Abuse and Neglect

Living with neglect or abuse makes the world an extremely scary place and can lead to a host of developmental and emotional difficulties. The effects of abuse and neglect depend upon their severity and duration, as well as the individual child. Extreme neglect and abuse can result in nearly complete withdrawal from any attempts to connect with others. Less severe cases can result in the child understandably and persistently seeking love and approval through chronic people pleasing. People-pleasing behavior is likely to be heightened among people who suffered neglect or abuse, since abused children are often willing to do anything to stay in the good graces of the abuser and avoid further mistreatment.

Reflection:
Exploring Your Childhood Wound

Gently settle in by practicing Mindfulness of the Breath, as described in chapter 1, for a few minutes. Then review the categories of childhood wounds outlined above to discern which, if any, apply to you. As you reflect upon these questions, remember to notice and let go of judgment of yourself or your caregivers as best you can. Was your caregivers' love conditional, and if so, what were the circumstances? Did you experience abuse or neglect that resulted in feeling unloved or unlovable? Did your parents sometimes withdraw their love and acceptance? If so, when and how did they do this? Were you allowed to explore what was important to you and participate in decisions? What feelings arise when you think about this? Take some time to write in your journal about childhood incidents that reflect any of these circumstances. How do those events affect your life now? This type of exploration can be painful, so please be gentle with yourself as you explore this topic.

Summary

When we are children, the greatest gift we can receive is to be loved exactly as we are. This is a major foundational aspect of psychological well-being, and we all desire it. Without this gift, our hearts are wounded and we cannot realize that our true nature is love. We naturally protect ourselves from being hurt again by closing off from our feelings, our bodies, and our innate wisdom. We develop a chronic sense of disconnection and come to believe that there is something inherently wrong with us. This makes it extremely difficult to give and receive love.

As a result, we develop an unquenchable thirst for love and a deep fear of not finding it—two powerful forces leading to a chronic pattern of people-pleasing behaviors. Life becomes a quest to find love, approval, and evidence that we're good enough to deserve love and approval. However, because people-pleasing behaviors are based on the idea that we must do these things in order to be loved, they actually deny us the experience of being accepted as we are. Fortunately, mindfulness and loving-kindness practices can help us know and feel our innate goodness, regardless of whether we received enough unconditional love earlier in life.

3

Chronic People Pleasing

The paradoxical quality of chronic people pleasing described in chapter 2 is so central to this problem that it bears repeating: Compulsively trying to earn love and acceptance doesn't work and actually leaves us feeling more dissatisfied and empty. As you read this chapter, remember that unconditional love is quite difficult to both give and receive, and that attempts to please others can never yield the experience of unconditional love precisely because the effort made to earn it means it isn't unconditional. Thus, all attempts to gain love and approval fall short of achieving the nearly impossible prize of unconditional love, regardless of how well you please others. Though this strategy doesn't work, however, the driving force behind it (the desire to be loved unconditionally) is understandable, and the state of feeling unloved is worthy of great compassion.

This chapter examines the thoughts, emotions, and behaviors involved in chronic people pleasing. Identifying those that are relevant to you will help you see your starting point: the place where your journey to freedom begins. I invite you to practice mindfulness as you read this material. Stop frequently to take a breath and notice your thoughts and feelings. In later chapters, I'll offer a variety of mindfulness practices and exercises that can help you work with habitual people pleasing and open to the love that's inside you so you can grace yourself and others with love that's more accepting, and maybe even unconditional.

Chronic People-Pleasing Thoughts

Let's begin with some of the most common thoughts involved in chronic people pleasing. As you read the following sections, remember the paradoxical nature of chronic people pleasing. Notice which of these thoughts you tend to have and any judgments you make about the thoughts or yourself for having them. It's important to recognize that many of our thoughts and beliefs are outside of our awareness, which makes them all the more powerful. Later, in chapter 6, you'll learn how to practice mindfulness with thoughts, and this will give you more choice in how to respond to them.

"I'll Do Anything to Be Loved"

To obtain the love you so desire, you may think you need to satisfy others no matter what the cost. This is the thought most characteristic in habitual people pleasing. You may mistakenly believe that if others approve of you, you'll finally obtain the unconditional love that you've always wanted. You may also worry that if you don't satisfy others, your chances of receiving unconditional love are slim to nonexistent and you may be abandoned. It's amazing what people will do to earn love.

"What Do Others Want from Me?"

Another common people-pleasing thought is characterized by compulsive worry about what others think about you, what they expect of you, and what you should do about it (Braiker 2001). You may go into overdrive worrying about others' desires and opinions and fixate your attention outside yourself. The supporting belief is that if you can know what others want and give it to them, surely they'll provide the unconditional love and sense of safety you desire. Looking at it from a slightly different angle, a goal of chronic people pleasing is to avoid displeasing others and creating any conflict that might result in love being withdrawn. In many cases, you may not even truly know what others actually want from you. You simply assume you know what they want and then go for it.

As a young adult, I slogged through the extensive, stress-inducing process of obtaining the education and certification required to become a Certified Public Accountant simply because I thought my dad and ex-husband, both CPAs, wanted me to. There are many less drastic, everyday examples of how we worry about what we should do to get others' approval—thoughts as ordinary as *I wonder what everyone else is wearing to the party* or *Geez, she's watching me again; I wonder what she wants* or *He's frowning;* or *What did I do wrong?* Such thoughts may have the worried quality of trying to figure out what others expect of us in order to give it to them and thus be loved or liked. These thoughts are also meant to keep us out of trouble by anticipating others' needs or expectations. For example, we may think that knowing how to dress can help us either gain or keep others' acceptance and thereby assure love and safety.

"It's Up to Me"

There are a couple of implicit assumptions that can influence your worry about what others want and what you should do to meet their needs. The presumption that people actually need to be taken care of sets you up for worrying about how to help them. The other main belief is that you are the one who should do the caretaking. These ideas can elevate your worry to new heights and fuel the fire of chronic people pleasing.

"I'm Not Worthy of Love"

You may hold the fairly common belief that there's something innately wrong with you—that you simply aren't worthy of love and therefore must constantly try to earn it (Rapson and English 2006). With these illusions in place, it's only natural that you would discount your legitimate needs and focus on others' desires. In addition, feelings of unworthiness can make you work even harder to prove your worth by trying to please others, an effort that also helps divert attention from these painful feelings.

"I'll Be Judged and Rejected"

In his book *When Pleasing You Is Killing Me*, psychotherapist Les Carter sums up one of the key thoughts involved in approval seeking: "People pick up the notion that they are doomed to be poorly judged if they do not act as others would want them to act" (2007, 107). You may think that criticism is a harbinger of rejection and therefore be acutely sensitive to it and possibly adept at avoiding it. You might try to preempt criticism by attempting to please others in some way, perhaps by being overly nice or solicitous.

In addition, you may compulsively scan the environment for indications that someone needs you or is upset with you and be acutely attuned to potential signals that this is occurring. You may interpret the rhythm and force of someone's footsteps as an indication that the person is angry and is really going to let you have it. You may think a certain tone of voice means the speaker is out of sorts and that you're responsible for that person's mood and need to fix it. The purpose of this hypervigilance is to help you avoid conflict or the disdain of others by either escaping or becoming a caretaker to prevent any further difficulty. These assumptions aren't necessarily true, and staying on hyperalert can be exhausting, especially if it routinely results in unneeded, anxious caretaking behaviors.

"I Must Be Perfect"

Another common thought process involved in trying to win love and avoid rejection is trying to be perfect and attempting to anticipate and correct any personal faults (Braiker 2001). Since it's impossible for anyone to be perfect, this becomes a grueling struggle fraught with endless, painful self-evaluation and self-criticism. Because some of this striving to be perfect results in positive results, perfectionism may bring about an idealized image of ourselves that masks feelings of unworthiness and shame. In the end, this leads to exhaustion and a paradoxical sense of failure, as it's impossible to live up to such a high standard.

Given the natural survival instinct to avoid abandonment and the common tendency to internalize our caregivers' criticisms, this kind of perfectionism and self-judgment makes sense. However, if you don't allow yourself to be seen exactly as you are, you can never be accepted exactly as you are. The result is a cycle of repeatedly trying to gain acceptance but never succeeding.

• *Chris's Story*

Chris, a forty-year-old bookkeeper and mindfulness student, who experienced what she called free-floating anxiety, had a moment of awakening one Saturday morning in her garden. It was a delightful spring morning, and the poppies were blooming. She was pulling weeds when she noticed tension in her body. She stopped and observed the tension in her jaw, neck, and shoulders. She also noticed that her attention had been about twenty feet away—focused on her husband, Charles, and what he must be thinking of her: *I didn't get that root completely out. I bet he noticed. He thinks I should be doing something else.* And then she wondered, *How can I be worried when it's such a grand day?*

This was an epiphany for her as she realized that the experience was emblematic of how she lived her life: always worried about what others thought; always thinking that there was something wrong with her and criticism was eminent; and always judging herself. This brought sadness—and also the thought that her worrying may have been unfounded. As she drew her attention back to pulling weeds, the same worry kept returning. Each time, she mindfully recognized it, took a breath, smiled to herself, and redirected her attention to the weed at hand and the beautiful day. This helped her feel calmer and allowed her to appreciate the moment.

Later, thanks to several months of mindfulness practice, Chris was able to see that her near-constant self-monitoring pushed her to strive for perfection, and that the pursuit of perfection, combined with her self-directed faultfinding, actually kept her from connecting with others and receiving the love she so desired.

Chris also became aware that she had difficulty deciding what she wanted. Because she was so accustomed to looking to others to determine what she should do, she typically excluded thoughts about her own needs when deciding what to do and how to be. The notion of focusing her attention in a direction other than on her husband was entirely foreign to her, and heightened because they'd never had children. The idea that her wishes might be as important as her husband's never even occurred to her.

With time and continued practice, mindfulness allowed Chris to stop in the moment and include herself and her needs in her estimations of what was important. At first she sometimes forgot to include herself, and when she remembered she felt tentative about doing so. But steadily she gained more freedom from the automatic assumption that only her husband counted, and in time their relationship became more balanced and rewarding for both of them.

"You Decide"

In the chronic approval-seeking cycle, if someone asks you directly what you want, you're likely to respond with whatever you think the other person wants or deflect the question back to that person. Even if you know precisely what you want, you may find it nearly impossible to express your wishes for fear of hurting others' feelings or offending them. The mind-set of chronic people pleasing makes decisiveness synonymous with acting selfishly (Carter 2007). You may have difficulty deciding where you'd like to go out for dinner, let alone uttering any choice aloud.

"How Do I Stack Up?"

Another insidious facet of an overzealous focus on others is frequent and unfair comparisons of yourself to others. These thoughts typically and unfortunately result in judging yourself as less than or not as good as others and may cause you to think that others are always better than you. In addition, you may begin to idealize others, further eroding your self-respect and self-trust and making equality impossible in your relationship. In essence, constantly comparing yourself to others erects another obstacle to loving yourself exactly as you are, making it more difficult to heal the wound of feeling unloved and unlovable (Welwood 2006).

"I Come Last"

If you deem yourself inherently unlovable and unworthy and have a near-constant external focus, this can fuel the belief that you deserve to come last and that taking care of yourself is selfish (Braiker 2001). When people begin to practice mindfulness, they often initially find it difficult to take time away from others to meditate.

One of my students, Rosie, a happily married mother of two young children, confessed that she wasn't practicing because she was so focused on her family that she seldom even thought about practicing. When she did practice, she felt guilty about taking time for herself, even though she felt more grounded and happier when she did. I helped her reframe her thoughts by engaging her in a discussion about how her practice might actually be good for her family. For example, if she felt more aware and grounded, she might be able to speak more kindly to her children and have more satisfying interactions with them and her husband—and vice versa. Seeing this allowed her to begin meditating more often. As Rosie continued to practice, she explored the thoughts and feelings that contributed to her original hesitation to devote any time or care to herself.

Reflection:
Exploring Your People-Pleasing Thoughts

Gently settle in with a few minutes of Mindfulness of the Breath. Then reflect on the thoughts commonly associated with people pleasing outlined above. Which do you identify with? Which thoughts aren't familiar to you? Can you think of any thoughts that are involved in your own people-pleasing cycle that weren't discussed here? Take some time to write about this in your journal, being sure to extend open-minded, compassionate, nonjudgmental attention to yourself as you explore these thoughts. To conclude, make a list of chronic people-pleasing thoughts that apply to you. Be sure to actually write out this list, as you'll refer back to it in later chapters.

Chronic People-Pleasing Feelings

It's natural and healthy to experience emotions of all kinds: joy, sorrow, surprise, anger, delight, disappointment, and fear, to name but a few. Emotions are an essential part of life, providing feedback about what's important. If you didn't experience fear, you wouldn't jump back if a dog growls when you offer your hand for a sniff. If you didn't experience profound grief at the loss of a loved one, you wouldn't have a sense of how very important that person was to you. If you didn't experience joy at the birth of a child, you wouldn't have a sense of how important family is to you.

Even though emotions are important, we tend to react to them by trying to get rid of those that are difficult and hang on to those that are pleasant. This kind of struggle creates a very challenging relationship with our emotions, and chronic people pleasing exacerbates this struggle in many ways. The following sections outline some of the emotions associated with chronic people pleasing. Some of them may currently lie below your awareness. In chapter 8, I'll offer mindfulness practices that can help you end the struggle with emotions and instead befriend them and shower them with kindness and compassion.

Anxiety and Vulnerability

A primary belief in the people-pleasing cycle is that bad things will happen if you don't satisfy others. Therefore, it's understandable that you may feel fraught with anxiety and vulnerability. The combination of vulnerability arising from the desperate desire for love, fears of not receiving it, and pervasive feelings of unworthiness and unlovability are a setup for pervasive anxiety. Furthermore, the desire for unconditional acceptance and the fear of being seen exactly as you are work in opposition to each other, creating an anxiety-inducing internal conflict. Because the natural reaction is to push difficult experiences away, most of these thoughts and feelings go unrecognized, which can prime you for more anxiety when they threaten to arise into consciousness. One way to distance yourself from these feelings is continuing to focus on others and what they might want or need.

When anxiety arises, we aren't in the present moment. When we feel vulnerable, our focus narrows in on the perceived danger, and we feel compelled to fight, flee, or freeze. Moreover, when we're aware of anxious thoughts and feelings, we often react with negative criticism toward ourselves, which intensifies our reactions. This is why it can be so difficult to extricate ourselves from the grip of anxiety and vulnerability. The future orientation, narrow focus, and negative criticism keep us in a reactive mode, especially in the absence of awareness. We may feel doomed to repeat old reactive behaviors, such as not speaking up for ourselves. Mindfulness can be so helpful here, providing the training that will allow us to dwell in the present moment, which is antithetical to anxiety.

Nancy, a seventy-year-old widow of two years with several grandchildren, provides a good example of how mindfulness can help with anxiety. When she first came to see me, she reported having chronic anxiety and said she couldn't see any reason for it. At one point, I guided her in practicing mindful breathing. Shortly after we began the practice, her eyes popped open and she declared, "I can't do this. I'm so worried about what you're thinking about me. I don't think I'm going to do it the way you want me to."

My heart went out to her, especially as I've often felt the same way. When we discussed what had just happened, it reminded her of how frequently she felt frozen when doing something for others. She said that she made all sorts of mistakes and blunders when people expected something from her, and that it had been this way as long as she could remember.

After a while, I encouraged her to try the practice again. I suggested that she acknowledge the anxious thoughts and feelings and, instead of pushing them away, simply shift her attention to the breath. Even within that first session, this helped Nancy feel more grounded and patient with herself.

Unworthiness and Shame

Thinking that you aren't acceptable as you are and being out of touch with your innate loving nature can lead to feelings of shame and unworthiness. The thought that you have to earn love holds those feelings intact and maintains your disconnection from your inherent goodness. Over time, these feelings become a filter through which you see all facets of yourself: every action, thought, and impulse. Of course, this negative progression only causes you to look at yourself even more critically and to seek external validation and approval even more desperately.

With this pattern, people often find their craving for attention and affirmation degrading and shameful. A sad example comes from my own family. My mother, Mercedes, was the youngest daughter of a large farm family, and while growing up during the Great Depression she felt unloved, unappreciated, and left out. She tried her best to be who people wanted her to be and do what others wanted.

As the youngest daughter, one of her chores was to carry the chamber pot upstairs every night. Afterward, her parents would kiss her goodnight and say, "Goodnight, little pot carrier." She never forgot the humiliation she felt about what she thought was a lowly task.

When my mother was in her eighties, she had hip replacement surgery. While helping her get dressed, I massaged lotion on her feet and legs since she couldn't bend forward to do so herself. She closed her eyes and reveled in it, and she told me how good it felt. I replied that she deserved a little TLC after her surgery. I could feel her whole body tense, and then she harshly replied, "*Nobody* deserves to be treated this way." It seemed that getting caught up in a moment of pleasantness elicited the feelings of shame and unworthiness and embarrassed her. Maybe she tapped into the longing for kindness that the massage fulfilled, and couldn't consciously react with anything other than disdain.

Feelings of unworthiness and shame will snowball in the face of the impossible task of pleasing everyone all the time. Even though you may know logically that this goal is impossible, that doesn't sink in at an emotional level because of how strong the underlying motivation is. Instead, you'll probably continue to expect yourself to achieve this unrealistic and unrealized goal, causing additional feelings of shame, guilt, and unworthiness for falling short of your expectations for yourself.

Anger and Resentment

Constantly trying to take care of others creates anger and resentment, and when left unresolved, these emotions can expand and become even more difficult to address. A client named Mary was a textbook example of this dynamic. A veteran caretaker, she had a full-time job, went to night school, catered to her husband's every wish, and managed their household completely on her own. Over time, the stress of constantly trying to please her husband and her boss while attending to all of her other responsibilities started taking a toll on her body.

When we began to work together, Mary told me that she wanted her husband, Bill, to help out more around the house but had never asked him to help and almost never expressed any anger about the situation. Meanwhile, she felt increasingly exhausted and frenzied about getting everything done.

As she spoke, I noticed that her face turned red and her body became rigid and tense. She also talked about how she had to do everything at work because other people didn't do their jobs and admitted that sometimes she felt unbearably agitated and enraged but didn't know why. Once she retreated to the privacy of her closet and ripped off her shirt, buttons and all. It was a brand-new, expensive shirt that she loved, and the fact that she destroyed it was what finally signaled that she needed to seek help. What upset her most was that she didn't fully understand the extent of her anger or the reasons for it. She considered herself to be irritable, but not angry.

As she started exploring her life through the practice of mindfulness, she opened to her feelings of anger toward Bill for taking advantage of her. She began to ask herself why she had squelched her emotions until they came spewing out in her closet. Gradually, she was able to bring compassionate attention to her experience and befriend the emotions she had fought for so long. Eventually, she was able to advocate for herself both at home and at work, and could do so assertively yet with compassion. With this approach, her anger toward others gradually diminished.

In addition to feeling anger toward others, as Mary did, you may feel anger toward yourself. This can result from saying yes to too many demands, contorting yourself to fit in with others, or shoving your wisdom, opinions, and legitimate needs aside (Carter 2007). It's understandable that you may feel anger toward yourself for not standing up for what you think, feel, and need.

Yet, as in Mary's case, you may suppress your anger (and other emotions) because you think you must be nice and pleasant at all times in order to please others. However, emotions will find an outlet. Suppressed anger is still there, and it will manifest itself in various forms, from physical ailments or depression to harsh self-criticism or passive-aggressive behavior toward others.

Even if you do express anger overtly, you may do so in a way that doesn't actually address the problem head on or resolve it. Examples of this may include road rage, yelling at children, or feeling angry because you have to wait in line at the grocery store.

Depression

Another difficult consequence of the childhood wound and suppressing emotions, particularly sadness, is depression (Braiker 2001). Of course, sadness is a natural part of life that can arise as a result of any kind of loss, big or small. Depression, which is more pervasive and chronic, involves feeling lifeless, stuck, and infused with unhappy feelings. Depression can originate from a variety of sources, including loss and grief, abuse, illness, genetics, and major life events, especially those that are stressful. Symptoms of depression include changes in sleep, loss of energy and interest in life, difficulty concentrating, significant weight changes, and perhaps suicidal thoughts. Some people say the difference between sadness and depression is that sadness feels mournful but alive, whereas depression feels leaden and life draining.

One reason for the sense of lifelessness typical of depression is that attempts to avoid difficult emotions generally result in dampening pleasant emotions too. Here's an example: Just like most people, you have the desire to feel loved. However, given that you suffer with chronic people pleasing, you fear being unloved and perhaps abandoned, which makes any relationship scary. Given this scenario, you might try to avoid getting too close in a relationship for fear of losing that intimacy, only to miss out on the joy of love. If you try to avoid difficult emotions, it's impossible to experience the pleasant ones fully.

It makes sense that chronic approval seeking can lead to depression, since they have several aspects in common. Both can originate from loss or abuse. Both can be fed by trying to banish painful emotions. Both thrive on negative thoughts, rumination about past events, constant worry, and self-criticism.

Many aspects of chronic people pleasing, including taking blame for everything that goes wrong, thinking that you always come last, and being disconnected from your wisdom and legitimate needs, can result in feeling unworthy, lifeless, and dead inside. Then, if you try to think your way out of depressed feelings or chronic people pleasing, you're likely to review other difficult and painful situations and find yourself even more imprisoned by negativity. This can feel like a hopeless situation. If this applies to you, take heart in knowing that mindfulness can help you free yourself from the negative thoughts that fuel depression and chronic people pleasing. It will also allow you to befriend the emotions that you've tried to suppress for so long.

Muddied Emotions

As mentioned in Mary's story, she sometimes felt enraged without understanding why. This is an example of what psychologists Susan Orsillo and Lizabeth Roemer (2011) describe as a muddy emotion, meaning it's neither clear nor understood. Muddy emotions can seem overwhelming and confusing. We don't know exactly what we're feeling; we simply feel upset or stressed. In addition, the experience of a muddy emotion may feel familiar and out of proportion with the situation, indicating that the emotion is linked to past events. In addition, we get so severely entangled in the feeling of being upset that it colors the rest of the day. Plus, we may end up fighting our emotions by criticizing ourselves for feeling as we do. Does this sound familiar?

According to Orsillo and Roemer (2011), emotions can become muddy for several reasons, all of which are aspects of chronic approval seeking. Emotions can feel muddy when we aren't taking care of ourselves. Mary certainly had neither the time nor the inclination to care for herself, so this might partly explain her confusion about what she was truly feeling.

Another reason for muddied emotions is what Orsillo and Roemer (2011) refer to as "leftover" responses, the result of not attending to past events and related emotions appropriately. This also applies to Mary, who never resolved her anger at anyone, especially her husband, and ripped her blouse instead.

In addition, unresolved painful experiences from long ago, such as abuse or harsh criticism, can make emotions muddy. These buried emotions can rise to the surface during moments that unconsciously remind us of painful past events. These feelings are extremely powerful, and because they are often outside our awareness, we tend to react with a plethora of behaviors that create more difficulty and continue the people-pleasing cycle.

Reflection: Exploring Your People-Pleasing Feelings

Gently settle in with a few minutes of Mindfulness of the Breath. Then reflect on the emotions commonly associated with people pleasing outlined above. Which of these feelings do you identify with? Which aren't familiar to you? Take some time to write about this in your journal, being sure to extend open-minded, compassionate, nonjudgmental attention to yourself as you explore these emotions. To conclude, make a list of the feelings you notice on a regular basis.

Chronic People-Pleasing Behaviors

Because we tend to go through life focused on the past or the future, many of our behaviors are actually unconscious automatic reactions to our thoughts, emotions, and physical sensations. In addition, many people-pleasing behaviors are either tinged or saturated with anxiety because the beliefs associated with chronic approval seeking are based in fear and the desperate desire to be loved. Although individual people-pleasing behaviors aren't of great concern in and of themselves, when they become a pattern they can contribute to immense suffering.

Just as with thoughts and feelings, gaining freedom from reactive behaviors requires that you become consciously aware of them. It's also critical to connect with what's truly important to you so you can make more skillful choices about your behaviors. The following sections outline some of the behaviors typical in chronic people pleasing. In chapters 10 and 11, I'll offer mindfulness practices that can help you choose your behaviors more intentionally, with greater compassion and less reactivity.

Doing What Others Want You to Do

All of the thoughts and feelings associated with chronic people pleasing come together to manifest in the overarching behavior of attempting to satisfy others even if doing so comes at a very high cost. You may reshape yourself in an attempt to do what others want or what you think they want. Many people who are veterans at approval seeking have done things that were either illegal, against their conscience, or not in keeping with their character, all in an effort to make others love and approve of them.

As you bend over backward to please others, even people you don't know well, you may get out of touch with your own physical and emotional limits and simply do too much. Your own self-care is likely to suffer as a result of an ongoing external focus combined with pushing yourself beyond your limits.

Chris, the woman who had the epiphany while weeding her garden, told me that she only attended movies that her husband wanted to see, even if they didn't interest her. Though this may seem minor, it was symptomatic. She chose friends she thought Charles would like. And without even discussing it with Charles, she gave up on her deep desire to have a child and pursued an uninteresting career because she thought (but never confirmed) that these decisions aligned with Charles's wishes. All of this left her feeling angry, unworthy, and disconnected from herself and her husband.

As Chris continued to practice mindfulness, she developed trust in her inner wisdom and felt more freedom to discuss her desires with Charles. Eventually, she went back to school and pursued a more fulfilling career. As both she and Charles took more conscious responsibility for their own needs, Chris realized that this way of relating actually afforded more respect to Charles than her previous pattern of acquiescing to what she imagined he wanted.

Mindfulness can help us become aware of the motivation for our behaviors as they arise. For example, Chris might notice that choosing to go to a movie that Charles picked was motivated by fear and anxiety about the results of not cooperating. With time and more balance in the relationship, on another occasion she might notice making a similar choice out of loving feelings. Exploration of our motivations and behaviors can help us gain freedom to choose wisely.

Jumping In to Help

If you make the assumption that people need to be taken care of and you must be the one to do it, this can certainly make you leap into action, especially if you're hypervigilant to signs that others may need help. When this occurs unconsciously, you may not see the situation clearly and jump in to help when the other person doesn't want or need help. People often want to take care of their own lives, in which case efforts to "help" are perceived as meddling or butting in. These behaviors can have unintended and painful consequences for both people. For example, having offers of help shot down may feel hurtful, while the other person may feel intruded upon and irritated.

Mindfulness practice can help us discern when and with whom caretaking behaviors are appropriate. Because mindfulness develops more conscious awareness, it gives us more behavioral options. For example, you might observe your impulse to help, then consciously choose to ask if you can help before jumping in. Alternatively, you might be able to simply sit back and do nothing. This isn't to say that unrequested help is never appropriate. Babies, children, and the elderly often need prompt attention, as do people in crisis situations.

Bungling the Job

From ages five through sixteen, I played golf mostly to please my father. I was always thin and small for my age and not especially athletically inclined. Still, the unexamined motivation to please my father was compelling, and sometimes I tried to whack the ball as hard as I could in an attempt to hit it long and straight. Invariably, with this approach I either missed the ball or duffed it a few yards down the fairway. But when I was relaxed, I could hit it long and straight for a child of my size.

Many people-pleasing behaviors result in the equivalent of duffing a shot. We try so hard to please others that we bungle the job. The combination of external focus and desperation to meet others' expectations makes it difficult to concentrate on the task at hand, paradoxically dooming us in our attempt to gain the approval of others.

Being Unable to Say No

Have you ever agreed to do what someone requested and later wondered what the heck you were thinking? For many chronic people pleasers, the word "no" is taboo, as it raises the specter of conflict. You may be so sharply attuned to doing what others want that saying yes is an immediate, reflexive response. It can happen so fast that you don't even realize that you have neither the time nor the inclination to live up to the commitment. Ultimately, you may end up feeling like a martyr, resentful toward the other person, and angry at yourself for mindlessly yielding.

Being Chronically Nice

In your effort to please others, you may put on a mask of cheerfulness, sometimes smiling through your teeth to avoid possible displeasure (Rapson and English 2006). This chronic niceness masks your vulnerability and desire for absolute acceptance. One of my mindfulness students, George, told me that a former therapist asked him to draw a picture of himself. The picture he produced showed a twisted smiley face surrounded by dark clouds. He told me that the smiley face was his way of relating to other people, and that the clouds represented his anger and resentment at having to please others all the time.

Taking the Blame

Another people-pleasing behavior is to apologize for almost anything (Rapson and English 2006). Sometimes you might take the blame even if you haven't made a mistake or done anything wrong. For example, perhaps you say "I'm sorry" to someone who bumps into you or apologize for not anticipating someone's needs. These apologies are often born of fear and are a plea for the other person to not be mad at you. Of course there may be genuine caring involved in an apology, but with the people-pleasing dynamic, fear and supplication are often dominant. These apologies allow you to avoid both other people's reactions and your own fear of conflict and abandonment.

Avoiding Conflict

Conflict avoidance plays a major role in chronic people pleasing (Carter 2007). This strategy for steering clear from situations that may evoke feelings of anger, hurt, and abandonment can show up in a number of ways. You might hold your tongue when you feel hurt for fear of the other person's reprisal. Maybe you leave the house if your partner is angry about something you've done. Perhaps you outwardly agree with another person's opinion even though you actually feel the opposite. Though avoiding conflict may seem like a good idea—and certainly less scary!—it can have severe long-term consequences. It prevents you from addressing and resolving relationship difficulties, and as a result they tend to fester and grow. So while it may seem that avoiding conflict would build harmony and closeness, it actually builds a wall between you and others as you attempt to sequester potential sources of conflict. I'll discuss conflict avoidance in detail in chapter 11.

Not Following Your Path

If you're focused on others, you're likely to be out of touch with your inner self. You may not know what you want, or if you do, you may not be able to speak up for yourself. Asking others to wait a few minutes before you attend to them may seem unimaginable. You may become tyrannized by this way of thinking and, as a result, tend to react to others rather than initiating activities that are meaningful to you. In other words, you may either shy away from acting in your own best interests or be unable to envision and choose your own way in life.

This was definitely the case for Chris. She was unable to discuss the possibility of having children with Charles, and she resigned herself to pursuing a career she didn't enjoy. Fortunately, Charles enjoyed gardening, otherwise she might have let that go too. Even so, she worried about doing it to Charles's standards, which sometimes denied her the peaceful feelings and satisfaction she found in gardening. This pattern of behavior deprived her of many opportunities to experience joy and meaning in life.

Withdrawing from Others

The sad and simple truth is that the collection of thoughts, emotions, and behaviors associated with chronic people pleasing, which were originally intended to bring you love and a sense of safe connection, often result in the opposite. If you're a veteran of chronic people pleasing, you may be so exhausted that you avoid other people so you won't be triggered to work hard to please them. If you've given again and again and have received little recognition for this, you may avoid other people for fear of getting hurt again.

Reflection: Exploring Your Chronic People-Pleasing Behaviors

Gently settle in with a few minutes of Mindfulness of the Breath. Then reflect on the behaviors commonly associated with people pleasing outlined above. Which of these behaviors do you identify with? Are any of those behaviors more prevalent for you than others? Which aren't familiar to you? Take some time to write about this in your journal, being sure to extend open-minded, compassionate, nonjudgmental attention to yourself as you explore these behaviors. To conclude, make a list of your chronic people-pleasing behaviors. Be sure to actually write out this list, as you'll refer back to it in later chapters.

Summary

The wound that cuts us off from our inner nature of love tends to elicit certain thoughts, feelings, and behaviors associated with the cycle of chronic people pleasing. Although this cycle is intended to achieve love and acceptance, it actually perpetuates the wound that caused it, exacerbating feelings of unworthiness and unlovability.

Reading this chapter may have felt rather daunting. The idea that chronic people pleasing affects so much of your life may be difficult to take in. Moreover, you may wonder whether it's possible to change something that seems so pervasive in your life. These are natural responses. For now, I ask that you hold them lightly and with minimal judgment as you read the next chapter, which explores how chronic people pleasing affects relationships. Then, in chapters 5 through 12, you'll learn many mindfulness skills that will indeed help you turn this dynamic around.

To free yourself from old habits, you need to take an entirely new approach. You can't use the tools and strategies that entrenched you in the cycle of chronic people pleasing to dig yourself out. You can't think your way out of automatic thoughts and feelings. Mindfulness, with its qualities of patience, compassion, and present-moment awareness, provides a radically new approach and a pathway out of simple reactivity and toward love and acceptance.

4

Chronic People Pleasing and Relationships

We've been looking at how your chronic people-pleasing tendencies affect you directly, but they obviously affect others and your relationships. Therefore, this chapter explores the impact of approval-seeking behaviors on partners and relationships. Because we are most vulnerable in love relationships, I'll focus on them. However, all other relationships are affected in similar ways, but often less intensely.

As you read, I invite you to come into the moment by taking a conscious breath from time to time. This may be the first step in establishing a practice that will later help you recognize relationship patterns and make new, conscious, and loving choices that nurture balance and connectedness in your relationships. Of course, it takes two people to create and maintain a relationship, so please don't assume all of the responsibility for any difficulty you and your partner might have—if for no other reason than because this can perpetuate the cycle of people pleasing and ultimately damage the relationship.

The Beginning

Kate and Jack met in college and hit it off right from the start. Kate quickly became focused on whether Jack approved of her and what she could do to make him fall in love with her. Jack didn't see this, but he appreciated how agreeable and nice she was. Kate conformed to Jack's desires, or what she imagined his desires were, and never let him see her in a bad mood. She didn't realize she was doing this; it just happened. She wanted to be loved, just as everyone does, but she had never felt secure in a relationship before. Her desire for stability and love felt desperate.

In fact, it was an act of bravery for Kate to pursue any relationship. She said dating made her feel nervous because she didn't know what her date wanted from her. When Kate was growing up, her father acted lovingly at times, but he verbally abused Kate if she didn't do exactly what he wanted her to do. From this, she developed the belief that others knew better than her how she should behave and that she had to meet their expectations to be loved. Until she really knew someone and what they wanted from her, relationships were scary for her.

An ingenious way to allow for love while simultaneously being scared of it is to idealize the other person (Rapson and English 2006), and Kate definitely did this with Jack. Of course, this strategy is flawed, as no one is perfect and we can never assure that we won't be disappointed or abandoned. In addition, it can perpetuate approval-seeking behaviors. Because Kate idealized Jack, she genuinely wanted to please him. Unfortunately, idealizing Jack was also like putting blinders on. Kate was so focused on pleasing Jack that she didn't know whether she actually liked him, whether he treated her well, or whether their values were similar.

For those with people-pleasing tendencies, the default choice in a partner is often a take-charge type of person, and this was the case with Jack. He always had things figured out and had strong ideas about where to go and what to do. Because Kate hadn't been attentive to how Jack treated her and because he had been on his best behavior in the early days of their relationship, Kate eventually discovered that Jack tended to be very controlling. As it turned out, one of the things Jack was attracted to was Kate's deference.

When painful early-life experiences have led one person in a relationship to develop a submissive demeanor and the other person to be controlling, the combination can produce an abusive situation. If this is the case for you, please understand that abusive behavior is unacceptable under any circumstances and should never be tolerated or blamed on the victim. No one deserves abuse.

Chronic people pleasing can lead to other scenarios early in a relationship, including an abrupt breakup. Someone with people-pleasing tendencies may enter almost any relationship in an attempt to feel loved. Meanwhile, the other person may find the people-pleasing behaviors irritating at best and bow out of the relationship. This can be painful and exacerbate feelings of unworthiness and desperation.

As Time Goes On

If the relationship does go forward, other types of problems are likely to emerge. The signs may seem subtle, or they may not make an impression on your conscious awareness. Since chronic approval seeking can leave you out of touch with yourself and your own needs, it's understandable that you may focus on satisfying your partner and remain unaware of any difficulties that are developing.

As the relationship continues and intimacy deepens, you're likely to become increasingly vulnerable to rejection. Fears of losing your partner may grow, and you may react by increasing your efforts to assure that your partner stays and continues to love you. This can result in you becoming the pursuer and your loved one, the pursued.

The wounding of the heart that fuels chronic people pleasing may cause you to disconnect from the body, which, as mentioned previously, is the place where you actually feel the sensations of love. When this combines with thoughts and feelings that you aren't lovable, you can be blind to the love that is present, leaving you dissatisfied and thinking it isn't enough.

The Unspoken Contract

If the relationship lasts, you're likely to go all out to take care of your loved one. In doing so, you create an unspoken, unconscious expectation that you'll be everything to your partner, do everything for her, and be who she wants you to be (Rapson and English 2006). Yet if you place all of your energy in the relationship, this creates unconscious and impossible expectations that your partner will reciprocate. In return for your sacrifice, you expect your partner to make you happy and provide unconditional love and assurance that you'll never be abandoned.

Unfortunately, the childhood wound described in chapter 2 makes it impossible for either of you to meet these expectations. Because this wound cuts both of you off from your internal, innate nature of love, and thus from feeling lovable, neither of you can display unconditional love. When this is combined with the expectation of unconditional love, no amount of love will be sufficient to make either of you satisfied. These expectations put a heavy burden on both of you and begin to erode the connection and intimacy you both desire. They may also breed bitter disappointment, anger, and resentment. The subtle and unconscious nature of the relationship contract adds to the problem, making resolution of unspoken disappointments unlikely.

Imbalance

When one partner is entrenched in people-pleasing behavior, the unconscious contract results in a precarious imbalance. You may do all the caretaking, and your partner may not be required to do much, if anything. In addition, you're likely to take a "one-down" position, abdicating your needs and opinions and not standing up for yourself. If unaddressed, this imbalance will continue to grow over time.

Your partner may contribute to this imbalance, especially if he has controlling tendencies. He may make unilateral decisions and become the authority figure in the relationship. If you have trouble making your own decisions, it may be a relief to let someone else take the reins. Yet it may also evoke anger and feelings of being left out and disrespected. If the imbalance continues, both partners are likely to end up feeling angry and resentful.

Saying yes to whatever your partner wants obviously contributes to the imbalance. Perhaps you readily took on all the household duties at first but have grown weary of these tasks. Meanwhile, your partner may have come to expect that things would be taken care of, leading to a sense of entitlement. Then, when the house isn't clean or the groceries aren't put away, your partner may feel angry.

All of the other typical approval-seeking behaviors discussed in chapter 3 feed the imbalance in the relationship. For example, saying "I'm sorry" for things that aren't your fault, perhaps even your partner's abusive behaviors, puts you in a "one-down" position. You may make excuses for your partner's behavior and conclude that if you had done better in some way, your partner wouldn't be upset. Of course, in all relationship difficulties both parties play a role, and as emphasized above, abusive behavior is never appropriate.

Remember Mary, who worked full-time, attended night school, and still tried to attend to her husband's every need? During our work together, Mary became aware of the anger she felt toward both her husband and herself for the imbalance in their relationship. We practiced kind awareness and compassion toward her feelings of anger and discussed options for how she might handle frustrations in her marriage.

Not long afterward, she had a chance to put her new approach into action. Arriving home from class late one night, she found Bill lying on the couch watching television and the house in disarray. As she mindfully felt anger arising, she took time to gather her attention, attend to her feelings, and offer words of compassion to herself so she could speak compassionately with Bill. Then, with tears in her eyes and fear in her voice, she told Bill that she wanted him to take on some household responsibilities. He actually laughed out loud. His laughter seemed to indicate his disbelief that she would dare to ask. It definitely reflected the depth of the imbalance between them. Of course, that isn't the end of the story. Fortunately, with the aid of both mindfulness and couples therapy, Mary and Bill were able to work together to find more balance in their relationship.

Avoiding Conflict

As mentioned in chapter 3, avoiding conflict is like building a wall between you and your partner. Although it reflects the desire to maintain your partner's love for you, it denies you the opportunity to resolve difficulties that can damage the relationship.

If you don't resolve conflicts with your partner, you're left with few options other than to swallow the related resentment and anger, further distancing you from one another. Also, suppression of emotions is a short-term solution at best. Anger and resentment are likely to seep out eventually, often in circuitous, passive-aggressive ways. You've probably had the experience of suddenly speaking harshly or acting unkindly and then wondering why you did so.

In addition, avoiding conflict deprives you of the increased intimacy that may blossom when you and your partner talk things out mutually and lovingly and find an acceptable resolution. Conflict resolution can be difficult, but it can help both of you release your anger and resentment and reconnect. Mindfulness can be immensely beneficial here, allowing you recognize the urge to avoid conflict and instead find loving and skillful ways to resolve difficulties with loved ones.

Avoiding Intimacy

The vulnerability that brings on habitual people pleasing makes maintaining closeness with others enormously difficult. Quite simply put, it's scary to be open to others when you're afraid of being hurt. In addition, the very nature of chronic approval seeking can get in the way of cultivating a close connection with anyone.

For example, chronic niceness makes it difficult for others to see you as you genuinely are. Your partner sees only the "nice" side of your multifaceted personality. In addition, when you bury your ideas, feelings, and opinions, your partner isn't privy to them, making it impossible to develop true intimacy. In short, not being real, present, and forthcoming about yourself prevents you from being seen, understood, and authentically cherished by your partner.

In addition, you may not see your partner for who she is. If you idealize your partner, you're missing out on the fullness of her humanity. Plus, if you assume that you must work hard to be loved or that you're unworthy of love, you may miss the opportunity to feel loved when your partner does express it. Likewise, if you assume that criticism is imminent, you may miss what your partner is really trying to say.

Other factors that serve as impediments to intimate connection include imbalance in the relationship, conflict avoidance, and taking the blame for everything. All of these can cause you to withdraw and lead to anger and resentment, which make it even more difficult to resolve anything. Then, if you end up carrying around old hurts for too long, you eventually might not even want to be close to your partner.

Formal Practice: Mindfulness of the Breath and Body

Set aside at least ten minutes or more for this meditation. As you develop your practice, you may choose to practice for increasingly longer times. Find a private place to sit where you won't be disturbed. Sit on a cushion or in chair, in a posture that allows you to feel grounded, comfortable, alert, and dignified. You may either close your eyes or keep them open, maintaining a gentle gaze on a fixed spot. (An audio recording of this meditation is available at www.livingmindfully.org/htp.html if you'd like to use it for guidance.)

Begin by practicing Mindfulness of the Breath for a few minutes, until you feel somewhat settled.

Expand your attention beyond the breath to include the entire body...from head to toe...from side to side...from front to back... getting a sense of the body as a whole. You may focus on the places that make contact with the surfaces upon which they rest... You may sense the envelope of your skin or clothing... You may feel an energy inside the body... Experiment with how you notice the entirety of the body. If you like, bring the breath into the background and breathe with the sensations.

As you focus on the entire body, your attention may be drawn to a specific sensation... Let your attention go to that sensation, noticing the qualities of pleasantness, neutrality, or unpleasantness of the sensation… As best you can, allow the sensation to be as it is and do whatever it is going to do as you gently explore it without trying to change or fix it… Letting go of any struggle to make anything happen. If a sensation is difficult, you can breathe with the sensation.

Notice the ever-changing nature of sensations…how they change in intensity and feeling tone…how some fade away. In a natural way, as a specific sensation fades or leaves the mind's eye, come back to the body as a whole.

Notice the wandering mind… Letting go of any blame or judgment… The mind is simply going to wander… When you realize it has, come back to the moment and the body. You may wish to gently label thoughts as "worrying," "fantasizing," "planning," and so on before returning to the breath and the body.

As you end this meditation, expand your awareness to include your thoughts and feelings. Then gently open your eyes if they're closed and turn your attention to what you hear and see, giving yourself some time to move slowly and gently back to the book or whatever is next in your life.

Reflection: Exploring How People-Pleasing Behaviors Affect Your Relationships

This reflection can be challenging, so you may wish to engage in the previous mindfulness practice to center yourself before beginning. Take a few minutes to reflect on what you've read thus far in this chapter. How did you feel as you read this material? Which of the impacts of people pleasing on relationships feel familiar to you? Which seem unfamiliar? Can you think of any impacts on your relationship not discussed here? Take some time to write about this in your journal, being sure to extend open-minded, compassionate, nonjudgmental attention to yourself as you explore this topic. You might also write about how you feel as you're writing on this topic.

Your Partner's Experience

It may seem as though being in a relationship with a people pleaser would be ideal. However, although your partner may reap some (or many) benefits from your desire to please and accommodate him at all costs, there are disadvantages to being on the receiving end of this kind of attention. The rest of this chapter is devoted to a brief exploration of some of these downsides. As you read on, please keep in mind that, as emphasized, both parties in a relationship play a role in any difficulties, so please don't take the observations below as an opportunity to berate yourself.

Feeling Trapped

Let's return to Mary and Bill's story. Bill liked being taken care of and enjoyed the many ways in which Mary demonstrated her love, especially in the beginning, so he unconsciously participated in creating a pattern of dependence on her. But over time, Bill started feeling indebted to Mary for her endless caretaking. He also felt guilty if he didn't entirely appreciate her efforts or got angry with her for any reason.

In their book *Anxious to Please* (2006), James Rapson and Craig English call this the "gilded cage," meaning that a person lives in luxury but lacks freedom. Part of the unspoken and untenable contract between Mary and Bill is that she would give up everything for Bill, and in exchange, he was supposed to pledge his undying love and support. Yet Bill felt trapped by Mary's need for his love and the caretaking she did to ensure it. This left him feeling contemptuous of Mary for her neediness and resentful and angry as he bumped up against the bars of his cage. He didn't understand why he had these feelings and often tried to quash them, but they leaked out in the form of belittling and demeaning treatment of Mary, despite the fact that he loved her.

Entitlement

When one partner takes care of everything, the other may develop the assumption that this is natural and the way the relationship works. In Bill's case, it simply didn't occur to him that he could pick up things around the house, wash the dishes, or do the laundry. As Bill became accustomed to Mary attending to everything, he developed a feeling of entitlement about being taken care of and became overly demanding and rigid in his expectations, sometimes either exploding or withdrawing sullenly when things weren't just so. Though this occurred outside his awareness, Bill felt entitled to being taken care of, partly because of what Mary unconsciously expected from him: perfect love. Yet because Mary was so kind, Bill felt confused by and guilty about his resentment, leading him to feelings of unworthiness and shame.

Suppressing Emotions

It took a lot of energy for Bill to live in his gilded cage. Much of that energy was devoted to an unconscious attempt to suppress his feelings of anger, resentment, contempt, and guilt. Over the years, these bottled-up emotions grew more intense, and increasingly, they came out in bursts without him knowing exactly why. As he struggled with his feelings, Bill experienced confused, muddied emotions, just as Mary did.

The Cycle Continues

In a partnership, each person's behaviors feed off the other's. When one partner has people-pleasing tendencies, a relationship dynamic is established that probably maintains the approval-seeking cycle and causes it to grow. As noted, Bill's feelings of entitlement and entrapment arose from an unconscious reaction to Mary's people pleasing. As Bill reacted with quiet resentment and made more demands of Mary, she tried even harder to win his approval, and because that didn't work, she felt increasingly unworthy and thought she was incapable of doing enough. This cycle created an increasing imbalance in their relationship, leaving Bill feeling more trapped and resentful and leading Mary to try ever harder to be nice and do things perfectly. Because much of this dynamic occurred outside of their awareness and both of them suppressed their feelings, they continued to avoid conflict and intimacy. The result was a downward spiral that left both of them feeling unfulfilled by their relationship. It's important to note that both of them influenced the chronic people-pleasing cycle and kept it going.

Sadly, what started as an attempt to assure love and a secure connection caused both partners to lose touch with themselves and each other, and to miss out on the kind of connection that's so important in life. This is inevitable when one or both partners aren't aware of the reactive thoughts, feelings, and behaviors that influence the relationship between them. Fortunately, mindfulness opens the door to the awareness and compassion that can free both partners to engage in the relationship in a more genuine, connected way.

Reflection: Exploring How People-Pleasing Behaviors Affect Your Partner

Gently settle in with a few minutes of Mindfulness of the Breath. Then take a few minutes to reflect on what you read in the second half of this chapter. Do you think your partner experiences the relationship in any of the ways described above? If so, which of these effects and responses seem most relevant to your partner? If not, can you identify other reactions to your people-pleasing behaviors? Take some time to write about this in your journal, being sure to extend open-minded, compassionate, nonjudgmental attention to yourself as you explore this topic. You might also write about how you feel as you're writing on this topic.

Summary

Although the intent of people-pleasing behaviors is to foster love and connection, over the long term these behaviors can have negative impacts on loved ones and our relationships with them. Relationships become imbalanced, yet we remain powerless to change this because of a strong drive to avoid conflict. Fortunately, we aren't doomed to relationships lacking in authentic connection. In the remaining chapters, I'll present numerous mindfulness practices that can help you explore and change your relationships, allowing you to give and receive love joyfully.

5

Coming Home to the Body

The human body is a miracle, but most of the time we aren't aware of it or the physical sensations we experience in the present moment, except perhaps when struggling with discomfort. We're like Grant, from chapter 1, who missed out on the fulfilling sensory experience of feeding his newborn son, Will, such as the feel of holding him, the smell of his hair, and the appearance of his tiny hands.

Much of our physical numbness comes from the childhood wound and the resulting desire to disconnect from the physical and emotional pain of feeling unloved and unlovable. However, because your body is your home and the place where you feel love, being numb to the body cuts you off from the love that might actually be available to you. Therefore, connecting with the body is essential to living in the present moment and healing. Cultivating compassionate, present-moment awareness of the body can help you inhabit it more fully so you can feel love, live more joyfully, and learn from the body's inherent wisdom. In this chapter you'll learn many mindfulness practices that can help you feel more at home in your skin.

Tapping Into the Wisdom of the Body

We experience life and love through the body, and it provides us with delightful as well as painful experiences. It allows us see awe-inspiring sunsets, hear beautiful music, touch the velvety petals of a flower, taste that first sip of coffee, and smell it too. We also see, hear, and feel our own suffering and that of the world. The practice of mindfulness begins with noticing sensory input, as in the mindful eating practice in chapter 1. In addition, being in touch with your body is a must if you are to take care of yourself. After years of tending to others to the exclusion of your own well-being, practicing mindfulness of the body will be important in your healing process.

As the book *The Mindful Way Through Depression* puts it, "If we can come to know sensations and feelings directly, befriending the sensory landscape of our own body, we will have a powerful new way to experience and be in wiser relationship to *every* moment" (Williams et al. 2007, 98). The body has wisdom of its own, and because our thoughts, feelings, and body are intimately interconnected, by paying attention to the body we can come to better understand the patterns of our feelings and thoughts. In fact, sometimes noticing the body can tell us more about our emotions than trying to analyze our situation can. Since the body stores emotions, paying kindhearted attention to the body can provide insight and help us open to our intuition.

Let's say you're worried about how to please someone. Perhaps your body tenses, butterflies flutter in your stomach, and your shoulders tighten. Yet because you're in a reactive state and probably disengaged from your body, you may leave these sensations unacknowledged or fight to make them go away. In so doing, you'd miss the wisdom of your body and its message to take care of yourself in some way. In addition, you'd miss the possibility of learning about and healing from the experiences that caused the upset, leaving you with unfinished business, deepening worry, and chronic stress.

Bringing awareness to sensations in the body can be difficult at first, especially if you tend to ignore it and your emotions. However, the steady, gentle practice of mindfulness can help you gradually connect with the breath and then the body.

Informal Practice: Coming Home by Noticing Sensations

At any time, stop and compassionately check in with sensations in your body. What sensations do you notice? Do you feel tingling, tension, coolness, or warmth? Simply notice whatever is happening without trying to change anything.

As you notice sensations and allow them to be present, you recognize and honor the wisdom of the body. This is what Chris did on that spring day in the garden, when she noticed body tension that alerted her not only to the current worry about what Charles was thinking, but also to how that moment was emblematic of her life. With ongoing informal practice, you'll become more sensitive to the body's messages and more apt to follow its advice.

Formal Practice: The Body Scan

The Body Scan helps foster awareness, compassion, and nonreactivity toward the body, which will enhance your ability to more skillfully address the difficulties that chronic people pleasing creates. The practice involves bringing gentle moment-to-moment awareness to the sensations in the body, experiencing those sensations with a spirit of exploration, and noticing the tendency to judge your experience.

As you're practicing, you'll probably notice that you often want the moment to be different than it is. When that happens, experiment with letting go of judgment and allowing things to be as they are, without trying to change or fix anything or make anything in particular happen, including relaxation. Trying too hard to relax can cause discomfort in your mind and body. The intention in the body scan is to bring openhearted awareness to your experience. Give yourself permission to feel whatever you're feeling without struggling with it.

The mind will inevitably wander away from the breath and body. This is simply what the mind does. Whenever you notice that the mind has wandered, gently acknowledge it, let go of any judgment, and come back to your focus. I encourage you to extend patience, nonjudgment, and kindness toward yourself and your body whenever you do this practice.

Set aside fifteen to twenty minutes for this practice. Over time, you may wish to extend the practice to forty-five minutes. No matter how long you practice, experiment with going slowly through the body as you pay attention to the sensations.

Find a place to practice where you feel safe and won't be interrupted. The body scan is usually practiced lying on your back in a place not associated with sleep. However, if you have a painful physical condition, your bed may be the only comfortable place; if so, please lie there. You can experiment to find which surface and position are most conducive to cultivating relaxed alertness.

Read through all of the instructions below, then practice the body scan. (Audio recordings of this meditation in various lengths are available at www.livingmindfully.org/htp.html, if you'd like to use them for guidance.)

> *Lie comfortably and gently close your eyes or, if you prefer to keep your eyes open, maintain a gentle gaze at the ceiling. When you're ready, create a gentle intention to be awake and aware... Notice the entire body, just knowing that you are here... Feel your body press into the surface upon which it rests... Breathing and noticing the entirety of your physical being.*
>
> *Now bring attention to your breath wherever you notice it most easily...the nostrils, the back of the throat, the chest, or the belly... Noticing the breath as if you've never noticed that you can breathe before. You may notice the mind wandering... Let go of any blame or judgment...and simply come back to the breath.*
>
> *After being with the breath for a while, imagine that your attention is like a flashlight and that you can beam it into different parts of the body... Beam your attention down through the left leg and into*

the toes of the left foot… Meeting the sensation in the toes with kind awareness… There may be sensations of warmth or coolness, tingling or numbness… If you notice the absence of sensation, that's okay too. The body scan isn't about feeling any certain thing but about opening to your experience as it unfolds—paying attention to what's happening and allowing it to be as it is. Experiment with bringing the breath into the background of your awareness and breathing with the sensations. This may not be easy at first. Experiment with it playfully.

When you're ready, bring awareness to the left foot… Experiencing sensations as they arise, linger, change in some way…perhaps the feel of a sock or an ache in the foot… Noticing any desire to fix or change what you don't like or hang on to what you do like… Allowing your experience to be as it is…not changing it in any way… Breathing with the sensations. When the attention wanders, return to awareness of the body.

Now beam attention up into the left ankle and lower leg… Paying kind attention to an ache, an itch, or the pressure of the leg where it touches the surface upon which you rest… Breathing with the sensations and practicing awareness of sensations in the ankle and lower leg as you did with the toes and foot.

Continue to scan the body, moving upward to the left knee and upper leg in the same way. Next, turn your attention to the right leg, working your way up from the right toes through the right foot, right ankle and lower leg, and right knee and upper leg in the same way. Next, turn your attention to the pelvic area, including the genitals, bones, organs, buttocks, and lower back. Next, scan the middle and upper parts of the torso, including the belly, chest, middle and upper back, shoulders, and shoulder blades.

Next, beam attention into the fingers of the left hand, then slowly work your way up through the left hand, the wrist and forearm, then the elbow, and then the upper arm. Next, beam your attention into the fingers of the right hand and notice sensations, then slowly work your way up the right arm as you did with the left. Finally, turn your attention to the neck and throat, then scan upward into the face and head.

Now notice your entire body…head to toe…side to side…front to back… Attending to the entirety of your body… Bringing the breath into the background and breathing with the whole body… Feeling the breath moving in the body… Being with yourself in this stillness…

Experiencing yourself as whole... Knowing that you have everything you need in this moment.

When you're ready, begin to make small movements such as wiggling your fingers and toes, paying attention to the sensations of these small movements. When you feel ready, attend to any larger movement you might make...perhaps a big stretch or rubbing your eyes... Begin listening to sounds around you... When you open your eyes (if they were closed), pay attention and really see whatever you're looking at... Give yourself some time to slowly move your attention to the outside world.

Stress

The body is incredibly resilient and can adapt to many circumstances. Even though we don't like feeling stress, these sensations are the body's adaptive way of asking us to pay attention. Unfortunately, we often ignore or push away these signals that indicate we need to take care of ourselves, and this can lead to health problems.

Stress arises when we perceive a person or a situation as a threat. Like other animals, when we feel threatened, the fight-or-flight response kicks in and a cascade of physical responses occurs. Adrenaline and cortisol are released, speeding heart rate, opening airways, slowing digestion, shifting blood flow to large muscle group, and boosting energy and muscular strength. If the threat is eliminated, the body will return to normal fairly quickly.

We humans differ from other animals in that we can elicit the stress response by simply thinking about a threat. Over time, perceptions of danger and attempts to cope with it cause chronic stress, as we contemplate the what-ifs and potential dire consequences and try to think our way out of the threat.

Hans Selye (1956), a pioneer in stress research, found that after a period of adaptation to a threat in which the body accommodates stress, it gradually becomes exhausted and prone to disease or chronic health problems. Stress can compromise your immune system and contribute to diabetes, muscle tension, headaches, heart disease, memory problems, high blood pressure, sleep problems, depression, and many other difficulties.

Informal Practice: Tuning In to Sensations of Stress

The next time you feel stressed, stop, take a breath, and notice the sensations associated with feeling stressed. Notice what sensation is most prominent. Perhaps you furrow your brow or tense your shoulders. Perhaps your breathing is shallow and rapid. Perhaps your heart races. Then, when you experience that sensation in daily life, use it as your cue to take a breath, come into the moment, and check in with yourself. You may feel irritated by sensations of stress and try to ignore or deny them. Instead, experiment with allowing them to be as they are and releasing any judgments. Simply letting go of the struggle may help you feel less stressed, and the sensations you experience may help you know how best to take care of yourself.

Jesse, who was trying to balance a demanding job, a happy marriage, and two active children, used this practice at work when he felt stressed-out. He noticed that when he felt overwhelmed, he had a tendency to clench his jaw. With time, he started to catch himself clenching his jaw even before becoming aware that he was stressed. Then, simply stopping to be aware of the sensations of clenching his jaw helped him get off of autopilot and tune in to how his struggle to do things perfectly affected him. He could then let go a little and breathe. In this way, Jesse found some relief and insight into his stress.

Chronic People Pleasing and the Body

Since chronic people pleasing is based in a deep longing to be loved and a fear of being unloved, it's understandable that it leads to stress and takes a toll on the body. If you've lost connection with your inner worthiness and beauty, life may feel like a proving ground for your value as a human being. The constant self-judgment inherent in chronic people pleasing further verifies thoughts and feelings of being unworthy. All of this creates stress that manifests in the body.

However, because your focus is fixed on others, you may not notice how this stress is affecting your body. Further, you may be inclined to deny or suppress difficult emotions associated with your people-pleasing efforts. Like many of the strategies associated with people pleasing, this is likely to backfire. Unexamined feelings are stored in the body, and if you try to deny or suppress them for long, you'll be like a pressure cooker that's about to explode. For example, resentment about always "having to" cater to others while disregarding yourself will simmer in the body, creating tension that must eventually be released.

In addition, maintaining the vigilance required to anticipate others' needs and being driven to please others both feed anxiety and further heighten stress. And like stress, anxiety afflicts the body with numerous physical symptoms including muscle tension, rapid heartbeat, elevated blood pressure, shakiness, fatigue, exhaustion, sweating, and stomach problems. If your focus on others prevents you from taking care of yourself by exercising, eating properly, going to the doctor when you need to, and so on, your health is likely to suffer.

Mindfulness can serve as a balm for this damage. Bringing kind, nonjudgmental awareness to sensations in the body can help you step out of people-pleasing situations momentarily and gain a little distance from them. Letting go of any struggle with these sensations will allow the body to serve as a firm foundation when the mind is spinning. This can help you access the wisdom to determine what's important in the moment. Here are a few informal practices that can help you tune in to the body and begin to care for yourself.

Informal Practice: Naming Sensations

When you find yourself in a difficult people-pleasing moment—perhaps being overly nice or saying "I'm sorry" when an apology isn't called for—stop and notice your body. Quietly name the sensations you feel, for example, "tingling," "tension," or "aching." Naming sensations provides a space in which you can practice letting go of struggle, be clearer about what is happening, and tap into the wisdom of the body.

Informal Practice: Noticing Your Energy Level

It's typical for people pleasers to take on more than they can handle. Next time you find yourself in this situation, notice what happens in your body. Do you feel changes in your energy level? Are certain physical sensations associated with feeling overwhelmed?

Informal Practice: Taking Time for Yourself

Find some time to take care of yourself during the day. Perhaps you might do a few gentle stretches, go outside for a brief walk, or sit quietly and enjoy a comforting cup of tea. As you give yourself this gift of time and care, what sensations are present?

Reflection: Exploring Your Sensations Related to Chronic People Pleasing

Gently settle in with a few minutes of Mindfulness of the Breath. Then think of a time when you felt hooked by approval-seeking thoughts, feelings, or behaviors. Perhaps there was a time when you were worried about someone's opinion of you, said yes but didn't want to, or felt resentful about doing so much for others.

Bring that time into your mind and allow yourself to reexperience it, capturing as many sensory details as you can. Where were you? What were your surroundings like? Were others present? After bringing the incident vividly to mind, notice what you feel in the body. You might quietly name the sensations, for example, "tension," "heat," or "pounding heartbeat." What happens as you allow the sensations to simply be present without fighting them? What is your body telling you? Extend kindness and compassion to yourself as you feel and explore your physical reactions. Take some time to write about this in your journal.

Formal Practice: Mindful Stretching

Mindful stretching can promote awareness and the attitudes of allowing, gentleness, and compassion toward your body and your life. Whether you practice yoga in a class or at home or stretch for fitness, you can bring these qualities to your stretches, transforming them into a mindfulness meditation. Just one caution: If you're unsure whether certain stretches are appropriate for you, consult your doctor before doing them. (Audio recordings of mindful stretching practices are available in various lengths at www.livingmindfully.org/ntp.html if you'd like to use them for guidance.)

As you stretch, bring beginner's mind to your body. Move slowly and gently, and explore sensations in the body as if for the first time. When the mind wanders, as it will, gently return to noticing sensations.

As you stretch mindfully, open to any opportunities to learn (or relearn) important life lessons. If a stretch is challenging, you may notice that you react with aversion. In that case, you can purposely welcome sensations of tension as an invitation to rest and find ease in the stretch. You may find that breathing with sensations helps you let go of any struggle against them and allow them to be present. The body's wisdom will inform you of its limits, helping you understand the difference between unpleasant sensations and pain and how to take care of yourself. It can help you know when you need to back off from a stretch—and when you need to back off from excessive attempts to please others.

The wisdom of the body can help you heal in many ways. When you stretch areas that hold chronic tension, buried emotions may be released. Don't strive to make this happen; just notice sensations in the body. As you tune in to your experience, mindful stretching can help you learn from the inside out that letting go and mindfully sensing the places where you feel stuck can help you feel freer, both in your body and in daily life.

For example, if your arms burn as you hold them out, you can gently challenge yourself to stay with the position for a few more moments, noticing the sensations and the desire to relieve the discomfort. Experiment with allowing the sensations to be present without struggling to change them, releasing into the posture. This can teach you that you don't have to react immediately to urges, and that sometimes they pass as you allow them to be present. In time, you can transfer these lessons to difficult approval-seeking moments, applying what you've learned about aversion, letting go, and not acting on urges.

Formal Practice: Walking Meditation

Walking meditation brings mindfulness to the moment-to-moment experience of walking. Typically, when we walk we're focused on getting somewhere, and not on the present-moment sensations of walking. In contrast, in walking meditation, there is no destination, and we bring our attention to sensations in the feet and lower legs. Although you can practice walking meditation at any time, it may be especially useful if you're experiencing strong anxiety that makes it difficult to be still for other types of meditation.

Set aside at least ten minutes for this practice. Find a place that's quiet and private and allows you a path to walk back and forth. You don't need much space—just enough for ten to twenty steps. Remember, you're not going anywhere; you're just walking. Feel free to experiment with the length of your path. You can walk at any pace, but slowing down will help you notice more of the sensations you experience as you walk. (An audio recording of this meditation is available at www.livingmindfully.org/ntp.html if you'd like to use it for guidance.)

Begin by noticing that you are where you are. Connect with your breath and then with the sensations of your feet on the ground... From a standing position, begin to take a step with the left foot. Notice the shift of weight from both feet to the right foot. Notice the sensations of the left foot coming off the ground...first the heel, then the ball of the foot. Sense how the pressure releases as you pick up the entire left foot. Experience the left foot and leg swinging forward. Then notice the sensations of placing the left foot on the ground again.

Bring awareness to the shift of weight from the right foot to the left...the sensations of the right heel coming off the ground, then the ball of the foot, and then the whole foot... Feel how the weight transfers gradually to the left foot as the right foot and leg swing forward to slowly begin another step.

Bring kind awareness to the sensations of pressure, the swinging of each foot and leg, muscle tension, touch, movement of clothing, and so on. When attention wanders away from the sensations of walking, as it will, practice patience and kindness. Let go of judgment and come back to the sensations of walking over and over again.

Summary

Since the body is your home and the place where you can feel love, it makes sense to pay attention to it and treat it with compassion. The body responds to chronic people-pleasing thoughts and emotions by becoming stressed. Cultivating compassionate, present-moment awareness through body-centered practices can help you inhabit the body and receive insight into your experiences. As you open to direct sensations in the body and let go of struggling with them, you can learn from the body's inherent wisdom, open to feeling love, and live more fully and joyfully.

6

Mindfulness and Thoughts

Remember Grant from chapter 1, whose anxiety took him out of the moment while feeding his baby? His story illustrates two major problems that arise from the ways we tend to relate to thoughts. First, he wasn't present to his thoughts and how quickly they affected him. His mind naturally went on a future-oriented mind trip that took him to a painful, imagined scenario in which his wife left him. Second, as Grant struggled to avoid his fearful thoughts and feelings, he judged them and himself and then immediately got busy by calling his colleague.

This chapter explores the nature of the mind, and how practicing mindfulness with thoughts can help us change our relationship to them. This allows us to cultivate a more independent perspective on our thoughts that offers more freedom from their emotional charge. Through this freedom, we gain the ability to choose skillful, compassionate responses to events rather than simply reacting to them. If Grant had practiced mindfulness, he would have had access to options for comforting himself, soothing his anxiety, enjoying his baby, and addressing his situation instead of avoiding it.

It's Not the Thoughts That Make Us Crazy

We all battle with our thoughts. We pugnaciously try to control them and their painful aftermath by diverting our attention from them, judging them as good or bad, denying them, or trying to think of something better. You may have noticed yourself struggling to think pleasant thoughts so you could be nice to others, or trying to get rid of self-criticism for failing to please someone.

Unfortunately, this struggle resolves nothing and actually makes it impossible to cultivate a mind that's settled and calm. Instead, battling with thoughts keeps us enmeshed in the stories we tell ourselves and the painful feelings and behaviors that result. In addition, the struggle to control the mind agitates it further, so we become even more entangled in the drama.

Here's an analogy you may find helpful: Let's say you discover your dog having a happy time chewing hungrily on your shoe. You gasp and grab the shoe to wrest it from your "best friend's" jaws. But the more you try to pull it away, the more your dog jerks back. Soon the ordeal becomes a battle of wills, with both of you feeling angry and increasingly determined to have your way. In addition, you may receive a bite from your friend. Analogies aside, the gist is this: What you resist persists. It's often skillful simply to let go of the fight, whether it's with your dog or your thoughts.

The idea of letting go of the struggle to control the mind may be difficult to understand and accept. It's so counter to our natural instincts to push away difficult experiences. However, through the active process of mindfulness you can learn to simply observe your thoughts without struggling with them and see your thoughts as events in the mind that are not you. This chapter includes several meditation practices that will help you experiment with these concepts.

Exercise:
Stop That!

First, let's do an exercise exploring the struggle to control the mind. For about two minutes, close your eyes and try to stop any thoughts or words from coming to mind. Remember, don't let thoughts come into your mind. Stick with this for the full two minutes.

* * *

Welcome back. What happened? Most people find that thoughts start popping up within a few seconds of trying not to think.

Gaining an Independent Perspective

One way to experience thoughts as events in the mind is to attend to them as you would sounds. In general, sounds are outside of us. They just come and go, and we don't take responsibility for most of them. In addition, when we listen to sounds we can get a sense of spaciousness, since sounds come from near and far away. We treat our thoughts quite differently. We take them personally and think we're responsible for them. We don't let them just come and go, and we tend to tense up around them. Listening to your thoughts in the same way as you would listen to sounds can help you take your thoughts less personally, feel less attached and reactive to them, and cultivate a more spacious perspective on them.

Extending an attitude of kindness and compassion toward thoughts is a key element in cultivating this sense of spaciousness and the ability to let thoughts come and go. For example, if you notice approval-seeking thoughts, you might try smiling and saying, *Oh, there you are again,* almost as if to greet these familiar thoughts. Kindness can contribute to independence from what would otherwise be a painful struggle.

Formal Practice: Mindfulness of Sounds and Thoughts

Set aside about twenty minutes for this sitting meditation. Find a private place to sit where you won't be disturbed. Sit on a cushion or in chair, in a posture that allows you to feel grounded, comfortable, alert, and dignified. You may either close your eyes or keep them open and maintain a gentle gaze on a fixed spot. (An audio recording of this meditation is available at www.livingmindfully.org/ntp.html if you'd like to use it for guidance.)

Begin by practicing Mindfulness of the Breath and Body, as described in chapter 4, for five to ten minutes, until you feel relatively settled.

Gently shift your attention from the breath and the body to the sounds around you, allowing your attention to open to all sounds. For about five minutes, just let the sounds come instead of searching for sounds... There may be sounds close to you or further away. You can also be aware of the silence between sounds.

You might notice that you have thoughts about the sounds, such as identifying or judging them... Notice that the sounds and your thoughts are different from one another, that your thought about a sound is not the sound... Experiment with letting go of thinking and noticing the sounds as though they are sensations...noticing the tone, volume, timbre, cadence, duration, and so on. When the mind wanders, acknowledge that and return to noticing sounds.

Gently shift your attention to thoughts as they come and go... noticing them in the same way you noticed sounds... Think of sounds as input to the ears and thoughts as input to the brain... Letting go of suppressing or denying thoughts... Letting go of hanging on to thoughts or encouraging them. No need to judge the thoughts... No bad thoughts, no good thoughts... Letting thoughts arise, linger, and fade away.

Notice when the attention wanders away, as it will. When this happens, simply come back to noticing thoughts. If the focus feels too wide at any time, you can always direct your attention to the breath. You might spend five minutes with this part of the practice.

As you end this meditation, gently open your eyes if they're closed and turn your attention to what you see around you. Give yourself some time to move slowly and gently back to the book or whatever is next in your life.

Informal Practice: Watching Your Thoughts

At any time, stop, take a few breaths, and notice your thoughts in the same way you did during the previous meditation, Mindfulness of Sounds and Thoughts, seeing them as passing events in the mind—events for which you are not responsible. This observation of thoughts allows for a pause between the stimulus and your reaction, helping you find more ease and freedom from worry and reactivity. Remind yourself that you don't have to believe your thoughts, and that your thoughts are not you. Practice patience and kindness with all you observe.

A mindfulness student named Camille described how the informal practice of observing her thoughts helped her while she was giving a business presentation. At one point during the talk, she realized she was worried about what her boss was thinking about her. She started to lose her focus, and that hampered her ability to speak clearly. She came to mindful awareness, took a breath, and acknowledged her thoughts. This helped her quickly refocus and return to speaking clearly and skillfully.

These kinds of results won't happen every time, and striving to make this happen can cause even greater difficulty. So the practice is to simply notice and allow. Remember, mindfulness isn't a practice of perfection, but one that gradually helps us find freedom from our habitual thoughts, including worries about pleasing others.

The Nature of the Mind

Understanding the nature of the mind can further your ability to let go of judging and struggling with thoughts. As some people say, the mind often has a mind of its own. Understanding this can help you see thoughts as passing events in the mind without getting caught up in their drama.

Monkey Mind

When Chris first started meditating, she noticed many things about her thoughts. She found that most of the time she wasn't aware, just like that day in the garden when she realized that her mind had been caught up in self-criticism and imagining her husband's disapproval. In addition, she was astonished at the sheer number and variety of her thoughts, including worries about what others thought of her and what she should do to obtain their approval.

She came to understand the metaphor that likens the mind to a monkey leaping from limb to limb and tree to tree. Similarly, her mind leapt from one limb to the next, from thought to thought, and pretty soon to a completely different tree, or train of thought. When she didn't tune in to her thoughts, her monkey mind continued to leap about until she was lost in thought and suddenly didn't know how her mind got where it was. Do you know where your monkey mind is right now?

Getting lost in thought and worry happens to everyone, but not being aware of the monkey mind leaping from limb to limb and tree to tree can cause problems. Chris's monkey mind leapt from the beautiful day and the activity at hand to her husband and his presumed criticism of her. As a result, not only did she miss out on the beautiful day, she also experienced feelings of inadequacy and anxiety as she compared herself to the standards she attributed to her husband. She also felt resentment toward Charles for his presumed judgment. With mindfulness practice, she could more easily acknowledge her worries, let them go, and enjoy the moment.

The Benefits of Presence

The difficulties that result from an unattended mind are illustrated in a study from Harvard University in 2010, showing that no matter where it goes, the wandering mind promotes unhappiness (Killingsworth and Gilbert 2010). The research, which looked at 2,250 subjects and 250,000 data points, showed that people's minds wandered nearly 50 percent of the time during their waking hours. The results also showed that people were happiest when they were focused on whatever was happening in the moment, including being happier than when the mind had wandered to pleasantries.

This study's results may be indicative of how the human brain evolved over millennia. We developed big brains to outsmart deadly predators and challenging environmental conditions. We ensured our species's survival and success by learning to hunt, collect, and grow our food. The mind developed exquisitely, churning out reviews of the past, plans for the future, creative solutions, and inventions, ultimately resulting in technological wonders like computers and the Internet—and helping us remember what to pick up at the grocery store.

Clearly, the mind is enormously helpful a lot of the time. But because it developed as a tool for survival, it almost never stops looking for trouble. The mind is always evaluating, analyzing, and worrying. For example, we constantly analyze what others think about us and expect from us, what we should do in response, and what will happen if we don't comply.

In addition, our thinking involves nearly constant appraisal of our experience and how we're doing. We evaluate unpleasant and painful experiences so that we can avoid them, and we try to plan how we can maximize pleasant experiences. For the most part, we believe that thinking will resolve things, but the mind doesn't know when to quit. This constant evaluating and judging can make it difficult to feel satisfied with life as it is, and it also keeps us stuck in chronic people-pleasing mode.

The solution is a no-brainer: Mindfulness is the antidote to the monkey mind. The simple presence of mind fostered through mindfulness can bring greater contentment by helping us notice where our thoughts are going and gain a less reactive perspective of them.

The Mind Thinks All by Itself

As you practice mindfulness, you may realize that the mind thinks *all by itself.* You don't even have to try to think; thoughts just arise, and they can be quite powerful. For example, let's say you notice that your friend has a scowl on her face and is speaking in a short, curt tone. Without you consciously deciding to think about this, the mind says, *Geez, I wonder what I did to upset her?* Perhaps this is followed by *I must have done something wrong.* The next thought may be *See? I can't seem to do anything right. I'm just worthless.*

Without your conscious awareness, your mind is simply weaving a drama of faultfinding and self-judgment. As this drama unfolds, you react to it, and a torrent of emotions and behaviors floods in. You may feel anxious, ashamed, and confused about what you might have done to hurt your friend. Through mindfulness, you can compassionately acknowledge your thoughts and feel a little freer from their potential drama.

It may also help you take your thoughts less personally if you know that everyone's mind generates thoughts without its owner's say-so. Early on in mindfulness classes, many participants are comforted when they find out that everyone else's mind also wandered during meditation.

Finally, keep in mind that because your thoughts arise without your bidding, your thoughts aren't your fault. Knowing this can help you feel greater independence from them and thus be less reactive to their content. Moreover, the less you blame yourself for your thoughts, the more willing you might be to take a look at them. Practicing letting go of blame for your thoughts can help you be less reactive during people-pleasing moments.

Informal Practice:
Grounding Yourself When Overwhelmed with Thoughts

When you feel overwhelmed with thoughts, give yourself a chance to regroup by grounding your awareness in sensate experiences. Precisely notice your moment-to-moment physical experience. For example, if you're taking a sip of water, notice your arm muscles moving as you reach for the glass, the feel of the glass as you touch it, the temperature of the glass on your lips, the feel of the water in your mouth, and the sensations of swallowing and the water flowing down your esophagus. Notice how you feel afterward. You may be more grounded and able to access a more independent perspective.

I have a vivid memory of practicing yoga a few hours before I was to give a television interview about mindfulness. As I practiced a forward bend, my attention anxiously went to how the presentation would go and whether others would like it. I switched my attention, over and over again, to the present moment, the breath, the sensations in the backs of my legs, my fingers touching the floor, and the feel of my neck releasing. This allowed me to feel peaceful, centered, and better prepared for the presentation.

Thoughts Are Not Reality

Knowing that your thoughts aren't reality is another way to take some of the sting out of them. For example, sitting here now, I can think of my white car in the garage. The thought of my white car isn't my white car. It's fairly easy to grasp that my car and the thought of my car aren't the same—that this thought is not reality. This can be harder with less tangible thoughts, like ideas about your worthiness. However, your thought that you aren't worthy of love is no more a reality than my thought about my white car.

Through mindfulness practice, Chris realized that her thoughts about her worth were not her, they were simply events in the mind that arose on their own. This awareness helped her lightheartedly breathe with difficult thoughts and greet them as they arose.

Things Are Not as They Seem

Sometimes we're absolutely convinced that things are a certain way when actually they aren't that way at all. We make interpretations based on a running narrative in the mind, which operates in the background and informs us about how we feel and what we do, like the operating system of a computer. These interpretations are influenced by our feelings and moods. Let's say that you wake up late, leave your lunch on the kitchen counter, and grumble at traffic on the way to work. At work you receive a voice mail from your partner, asking you in an exasperated tone of voice to call him. What would you be thinking and feeling?

Now imagine that you woke up on time and made it to work with your lunch, having navigated traffic easily. You hear a message from your loved one asking you, in an exasperated voice, to call him. Given this scenario, what would you be thinking and feeling?

Like most people, your interpretations and predictions about the message would vary depending upon your state of mind and emotion. On a difficult day you might think your loved one is feeling angry toward you and then worry about what's up. You might think, *Geez, I wonder what I did this time?* On an ease-filled day, you might think, *Ah, he sounds upset. I hope he's all right.* So which interpretation is the truth?

Mindfulness can help us be present, take a breath, and notice our frame of mind, interpretations, and assumptions. When we consciously acknowledge these thoughts and mind states, we have a greater chance of not tripping down the trail of worry and dread. Instead, we can remind ourselves to let go, let be, and see what happens.

You Don't Have to Believe Everything You Think

Often, we're unaware of our assumptions and therefore unable to question them or the fact that we think they're correct. We simply react as if they're true. Some of the assumptions in the chronic approval-seeking cycle are that we must always please others, that we aren't worthy of love, and that we must be perfect. Even though these assumptions aren't real or true, they rule us when we don't attend to them.

In a mindfulness class, Sophia, a twenty-seven-year-old graduate student in geology, reported an unsettling event. Her neighbor, Alicia, had called her to ask for help with something. Sophia wasn't in, so Alicia left a message. Sophia felt embarrassed and ashamed that she didn't get the message until it was too late to respond. Her thoughts spun: *What will she think of me? She must think I wanted to get out of helping her. She's going to ditch me.*

For several days Sophia avoided Alicia, trying to steer clear of her friend's possible anger and disappointment. Sophia had come to value her comfortable conversations with Alicia and didn't want her to end the friendship. Then, by chance, Sophia bumped into Alicia at the grocery store. She was astonished that Alicia not only wasn't upset with her, but was genuinely delighted to see her. As proof of this, Alicia even invited Sophia to a gathering with other friends. This was a moment of awakening for Sophia. Things were not as she thought; in fact, they were actually quite the opposite.

This turn of events caused Sophia to being to question her assumptions. A bit sadly, she started to wonder, *I thought I had to earn Alicia's friendship. That's a lot like how I thought I had to earn love from Mom and Dad. What if I've been wrong all this time? What if people like me just as I am? What if I've had love around me for years and couldn't see it?*

As we worked together, Sophia began to acknowledge and let go of the struggle with her perceptions about needing to earn love and became aware of the interplay between her thoughts and feelings. In addition, she began to notice that her mind had a mind of its own and that her thoughts were not facts. Sophia brought patience and persistence to this awareness process, and gradually it helped her be kind and nonjudgmental with self-critical and fearful thoughts and see them as simply events in the mind.

Thoughts Are Impermanent

Another way to relate to thoughts is to see them as the impermanent objects of the mind that they are. During meditation, experiment with observing thoughts come and go. Let them flow through the mind without trying to control them. It can be helpful to imagine the mind to be as big as the vast blue sky and thoughts to be like clouds just passing by.

Of course, there are cloud thoughts of all kinds. As you watch thoughts during meditation, you can notice that some are like wispy clouds, floating through the sky of the mind without obscuring it for long. Thoughts like *What a beautiful day* or *What should I have for lunch?* come and go easily. Other thoughts are like heavy, overcast clouds that cast a shadow for what seems to be an eternity. Some people-pleasing thoughts can certainly loom like dark clouds—for example, *I'm completely worthless* or *I just can't please him* or *Why did I say that to her? She'll think I'm horrible.*

However, like all clouds, all thoughts come and go. Mindfulness can help cultivate the qualities of nonattachment and patience, allowing you to observe thoughts, wispy or dark, as they pass through in the mind.

Working with Chronic Approval-Seeking Thoughts

Because chronic people-pleasing thoughts are fueled by fear, they consume a lot of energy and time, and it may be difficult to see them as passing mental events. Experiment with reminding yourself of what you've read thus far in this chapter. Bear in mind that the process of noticing and allowing will be refined as you continue to practice. This can help you practice again and again and again, trusting that this practice, which is simple but not easy, can lead to freedom.

Exercise: Label Your Thoughts

Take a look at the list of your people-pleasing thoughts from chapter 3 and add any others you've thought of since making the list. Next, review your list and identify your recurrent thought patterns. Then come up with a name or label for each pattern of thought. For example, thoughts like *I'm such an idiot* or *It's all my fault* could be named "blaming thoughts." Thoughts like *How can I make her like me?* or *I have to say yes* could be named "approval-seeking thoughts." Use these names as you experiment with the following informal practices, which can aid the process of observing and letting go.

Informal Practice: Labeling Thoughts in the Moment

When a thought from your list arises, acknowledge and label it. This will help you create a little distance from the thought, step out of the drama, and rob it of some of its power over you. Eventually, you can smile at the thought and say, *Ah, there you are.*

Informal Practice: Noticing Your People-Pleasing Focus

Come into the present moment and notice whether you're focused on or simply thinking about someone else. Through kind awareness, you may realize that any such thoughts have a people-pleasing quality. Observe your thoughts. Are you wondering if someone would like what you're doing in the moment or what someone thinks of you? Are you trying to figure out how you can please someone or assuming that others are silently criticizing you? Without fighting with such thoughts, experiment with refocusing on your internal experience and asking yourself, *What needs my attention right now?* This can help you take charge of the habit of attending to everyone else and excluding yourself. In this way, you can retrain your thoughts to be more balanced and respectful of your needs and what's important to you. This practice has been an important teacher for me. I hope it's helpful for you.

Underneath It All

Let's revisit Sophia, who was shocked to find that her friend Alicia loved her even when she hadn't been able to provide the help that Alicia requested. As Sophia continued practicing mindfulness, she became aware of the feelings of unworthiness and fear that lurked beneath the surface of her awareness and fueled chronic approval-seeking thoughts, such as *I wonder what she thinks of me*, *I just hate myself*, and *I don't fit in. What should I do?* These kinds of thoughts are the tip of the iceberg that can alert you to the large, submerged mass beneath: painful feelings (Williams et al. 2007).

By tuning in to her thoughts, Sophia began to engage in an essential part of the healing process: opening to feelings that lay beneath those thoughts—emotions that were attached to unfinished business and old memories of her parents withdrawing signs of love and heaping criticism on her when she made mistakes. Given the painful nature of these emotions, Sophia found that during meditation she often wanted to force her attention back to the breath and blot out her feelings. However, she felt lighter and more alive when she befriended her emotions by using some of the practices you'll learn in chapter 8.

Summary

This chapter explored how we tend to relate to our thoughts and how struggling with and judging them brings us difficulty. It also examined how conscious awareness can help us let go of this battle and relate to thoughts as events in the mind. With continued practice of formal mindfulness meditation and informal mindfulness in daily life, you can develop a more nonjudgmental, openhearted awareness of your thoughts, which robs them of their power to rule you. In this way, you can free yourself from chronic people-pleasing reactivity and have more choice about your behaviors. Remember that patience and nonstriving will help you stay with your practice and allow it to strengthen your ability to find an independent perspective.

7

Connecting with Your Inner Loveliness

Whether you call it Christlike nature, Buddha-nature, or innate loveliness, your essential nature of love is always present even if it seems obscured, as when fog clouds your vision of what's right in front of you. Chronic people pleasing is like the fog, blocking out the light of your true nature as a result of years of focusing on others and squelching your wisdom, emotions, and deepest values. When you understand that you are made of love, some of the fog of chronic people pleasing lifts, allowing you to see and directly experience your own goodness. This can heal the wound that kept you from experiencing your innate loveliness in the first place.

This chapter explores how you can reconnect with your innate loveliness. As you water the seeds of love within you, you'll be better able to accept yourself exactly as you are, imperfections and all. You'll be able to give yourself the acceptance you didn't get enough of earlier in life. As you acquire a more flexible sense of yourself, you'll feel more contented, more easily satisfied, and less afraid. In addition, you'll have a greater sense of belonging, allowing you to open to others authentically.

In this chapter you'll learn loving-kindness meditation. This, in combination with your ongoing mindfulness meditation practice, will be invaluable in rediscovering the love and goodness at the core of your being—qualities that remain untouched regardless of whether others love or approve of you. These practices will dispel the fog so you can finally find your way home.

We've All Got It

Everyone has innate loveliness—everyone!—and accessing internal beauty is transformative. Consider the movie *Dead Man Walking* (based on a true story), in which a death-row convict, Matthew Poncelet, and a Catholic nun, Sister Prejean, form a deep and resilient spiritual friendship. Near the end of the movie, after a long struggle with his horrific crimes, Matthew experiences that even he is a child of God and has innate loveliness, and with this realization, he is transformed. Suddenly his face is soft and joyful, rather than hardened, angry, wounded, and defensive, as it had been throughout. Seeing Matthew so radically transformed, the demeanor of most people who watched the movie changed as well.

Mindfulness and loving-kindness practice can help you foster the awareness that you also have this innate loveliness, and that you have it at all times, including when it seems to be buried or nonexistent. Even if you weren't raised to know that you are made of love, you can teach yourself your innate goodness. With this awareness you can open more joyfully to your life, accept yourself as you are, connect more deeply with others, act more assertively and intentionally, and find balance between caring for yourself and others. As with other aspects of mindfulness, this change is gradual and will grow from dedicated practice.

Informal Practice: Reminding Yourself of Your Inner Loveliness

When you get caught in the cycle of chronic approval seeking, remind yourself that there is more to you—that you have value, worth, and loveliness entirely aside from any efforts to please others. This is a way of gifting yourself with what you needed as a child. Even if you don't believe it at first, keep reminding yourself of this. Doing so affirms your intention to be kind to yourself and heal yourself.

Tapping Into Your True Nature Isn't Selfish

It's important to understand that tapping into your true nature isn't egotistical or selfish. In fact, by opening to your true nature you will become less self-involved and more allowing of your imperfections. This will help you experience others' inner loveliness and accept them and their weaknesses. As you come to realize that everyone shares this innate loveliness, you'll feel that you're part of something larger than yourself. In addition, when you feel secure in who you are, you'll be less reliant on others because you'll know you already have what you need.

The Truth Beyond Judgment

Mindfulness practice is key in connecting with your natural loveliness, helping you see beyond your judgments and perceptions about yourself. As you foster an independent perspective on your thoughts and judgments by relating to them as events in the mind, you'll see that your thoughts about yourself aren't who you are. This allows you to soften around judgments about yourself and promotes acceptance of yourself as you are: your quirks, your useful and not so useful attributes, your emotions, and everything that lies beneath the mask of chronic niceness, including your inner loveliness. With this more flexible view of yourself, you'll feel less defensive and more at one with the flow of life.

Let's say that after helping a friend, you think that you didn't do enough. That thought holds implicit judgment (*I didn't do enough*), but in addition, you're likely to judge yourself (*I'm a bad friend* or *I'm lazy* or *I'm not a caring person*). However, these judgments are simply events in the mind; they aren't indications of who you are. With this perspective on your thoughts and a more flexible view of yourself, you can extend more tolerance and acceptance to yourself, rather than heaping on shame and unworthiness. Knowing that you are more and less than your perceptions about yourself is freeing.

Informal Practice: Noticing Self-Judgment

At any time, take a breath and notice whether you're judging yourself. If you are, let it go as best you can. Also let go of judgment about judging yourself! Doing this informal practice regularly can help you be clearer about your true nature and more compassionate toward yourself.

True Nature and True Intentions

Through ongoing practice of mindfulness and loving-kindness meditation, we find that, at the heart of everything, we have deep intentions to help ourselves be happy and relieve suffering—our own and that of others. Further, we find that these intentions are the basis for everything we do. Knowing this, we take yet another step toward the truth of our goodness.

There were times in my life when I made unconscious, painful choices. One such decision was to get married at the age of eighteen. After that marriage ended, I felt anger toward myself for walking down the aisle. Through mindfulness and the loving direction of a skilled therapist, I realized that this decision had been motivated by the strong desire to find love in the midst of a harsh environment. I also saw that I'd married so young because I feared losing my fiancé if I didn't marry him then. Moreover, I understood that at the core of this decision was an intention to be loved and free from suffering—an understanding that enabled me to forgive myself for that decision.

As discussed throughout this book, many of the ways we cope with the fear of not being loved can cause great suffering, just like my decision to marry so young. As children, we learned these problematic coping strategies, such as saying yes when we don't want to, being untrue to ourselves in an effort to fit in, or burying our emotions. They are deeply ingrained, and we don't consciously decide to think, feel, or act in these ways. Even when we're aware of these coping mechanisms, the motivations behind them are strong, and sometimes we reflexively turn to them even when we intend otherwise. However, these coping strategies aren't our fault. They are simply unconscious, ingrained reactions.

Changing these habits is difficult, but it is possible. When you find yourself in the midst of approval seeking, take a breath and remember that your people-pleasing habits arise from a deep intention to help yourself be happy and free. Also let go of any blame or self-judgment for these habitual behaviors and ways of thinking. This can help you heal the wound that led to the difficulty in the first place. Psychologist Tara Brach, who teaches mindfulness in Washington, DC, says that forgiving yourself and letting go of shame about your coping strategies is essential in healing the core wounds from which the coping strategies arose (2011).

Mindfulness practice helps us cultivate the awareness, patience, and compassion we need in order to know and let go of our judgmental thoughts, forgive ourselves over and over again, and claim our own goodness. In these ways, mindfulness helps us gradually come home to ourselves.

Reflection: Creating Loving Intentions

Touch the moment by practicing Mindfulness of the Breath and Body for five to ten minutes. When you feel settled, state one or more loving intentions toward yourself. For example, one of my clients told me that her intention was to deeply honor her own good nature. Another client said her intention was to respect and trust her inner wisdom. What are your intentions? Take a few minutes to explore your intentions and write them in your journal.

Informal Practice: Reminding Yourself of Loving Intentions

Throughout the day, remind yourself of the loving intentions that you wrote in your journal. These reminders can help you make the choice to treat yourself with kindness more often.

Informal Practice: Reminding Yourself of Your Deepest Intention

When you find yourself engaged in a people-pleasing behavior that you're trying to stop, you might feel frustrated or angry with yourself. Acknowledge those feelings, allow things to be as they are, and then remind yourself that the deep intention motivating the behavior is to find happiness and freedom from suffering. This may help you be less harsh with yourself.

Loving-Kindness Meditation

Given the powerful impact of the fear and feelings of unworthiness associated with chronic approval seeking, you could use a big dose of kindness to comfort yourself. Loving-kindness meditation, which has mindfulness as its foundation, can provide just that. In the words of Sharon Salzberg, best-selling author and renowned meditation teacher, loving-kindness is the "ability to embrace all parts of ourselves, as well as all parts of the world" (1995, 27).

Loving-kindness is practiced by first directing love and friendliness toward ourselves and then extending those feelings outward toward others. Because habitual people pleasing normally locks our attention on others, for the purposes of this book we'll focus on loving-kindness toward ourselves. However, I encourage you to eventually engage in the full practice. You can find complete instructions for loving-kindness meditation in Sharon Salzberg's book *Lovingkindness: The Revolutionary Art of Happiness* (1995), among others.

Loving-kindness can be practiced in both formal and informal ways. Formal practice consists of repeating kind wishes during a period of sitting or walking meditation. Informal practice involves repeating those blessings to yourself during the day or simply beckoning kind feelings, especially when difficulty arises. You can also foster loving-kindness by reminding yourself of your intention to be loving and kind throughout the day.

According to Buddhist tradition, loving-kindness practice was originally prescribed to a group of monks as a remedy for their fear of living and meditating in a dark, haunted forest. In light of this story, it makes sense to muster the power of loving-kindness when you feel afraid to say no or anxious when you think someone doesn't like or love you. Moreover, loving-kindness helps channel the attitude of acceptance also cultivated by mindfulness in general. This quality of acceptance allows the mind to be spacious enough to hold all of life in kindness. In her book *Happiness Is an Inside Job*, psychotherapist and mindfulness teacher Sylvia Boorstein referred to loving-kindness as "sweetening the mind" (2008, 81).

Most of the time in our society, love is based on certain conditions being met. For example, if your partner brings home an expensive new purchase without consulting you, you may give him the cold shoulder for quite a while. Many of us with people-pleasing tendencies experienced the withdrawal of love by parents if we didn't meet their expectations. In contrast, in loving-kindness love is given freely and unconditionally. In fact, in the full practice, loving-kindness is eventually extended to "difficult ones," or people with whom you are in conflict. You may be skeptical about whether it's truly possible to extend this unconditional love to yourself and others. Try to let go of judgment and just see for yourself. It takes patience and time, but as you persist with loving-kindness meditation, you will experience that it is possible to love in an unconditional way.

Watering Your Garden

Some people liken loving-kindness meditation to watering seeds in a garden—in this case, the seeds of unconditional love. Harsh judgments, feelings of worthlessness, and a constant external focus are weeds in that same garden. I imagine chronic people pleasing as a garden in which the weeds have been watered but the seeds of loving-kindness remain dry.

When you water the seeds of loving-kindness that are already in you, you cultivate the capacity to let your love grow and eventually blossom. However, all seeds take time and tending to germinate, grow, and bear fruit, and too much focus on the end-product is unproductive. Remember that you're simply watering seeds and that they will bear fruit in time.

Also, be aware that there is nothing in particular that needs to happen during loving-kindness meditation, including feeling a particular way. In fact, it's best to let go of expecting anything to happen during the practice. Focus instead on the simple act of watering the seeds. That's all.

After years of devoting so much attention to what others want, it may feel selfish or difficult to direct love toward yourself. You may also find that feelings of unworthiness, anger, or guilt emerge as you practice loving-kindness. Simply offer kindness to yourself for those difficult feelings. In this practice, and in daily life, you always start in the present, right where you are, unpleasant feelings and all. Patience is also an ally when negative self-judgment or feelings of unworthiness arise.

Later in this chapter, I'll discuss how to handle and befriend the "negatives" that sprout up during loving-kindness meditation. For now, I'll just say that it is vital to consistently remind yourself that the power of love cannot be overcome.

Formal Practice: Loving-Kindness Meditation

Set aside about twenty minutes for this practice, and find a quiet, comfortable place to sit. You may find it helpful to set the mood by accessing feelings of love before beginning the formal meditation. You might stroke your pet, tune in to music or poetry, or remember a specific time when you felt genuinely loved. This isn't required, but it is sometimes helpful. (An audio recording of this meditation is available at www.livingmindfully.org/ntp .html if you'd like to use it for guidance.)

Begin by practicing Mindfulness of the Breath for a few minutes. When you feel settled, remind yourself of your intention to help yourself to be free from suffering.

Call to mind a being, human or otherwise, who makes you smile and whom you love a lot. If you can't think of such a being, you can imagine someone you don't know but who embodies love, perhaps Jesus, the Dalai Lama, Gandhi, Mother Teresa, or Martin Luther King Jr. Imagine that you are in the presence of this being now. Allow yourself to feel this being's presence. Notice what happens in the body, perhaps feelings of lightness or gladdening of the heart. See this particular being through the eyes of love. Sit for a few moments, relishing this imagined presence.

Now turn your eyes of love toward yourself. Notice your experience as you do so, remembering that nothing special needs to happen. Simply notice whatever happens inside you. You are watering seeds of love toward yourself, not trying to force them to grow and blossom right away.

Quietly repeat the following blessings to yourself for about fifteen minutes or for whatever time you have. Experiment with allowing gentleness and kindness to inform the way in which you speak to yourself as you say these phrases:

May I be free from fear and suffering.

May I have physical well-being.

May I have mental well-being.

May I be happy and truly free.

During this practice you may experience a variety of feelings. Respond to all of them with awareness, love, and kindness. Check in with your feelings as you repeat the statements. Experiment with acknowledging your feelings and allowing them to be present. If you find it impossible to express loving-kindness toward yourself, offer it to a loved one first and then come back to wishing yourself well.

You may notice a strong desire to acquire a sense of loving presence, and this is okay. When this happens, notice it and then let go of trying to make anything happen. You might remind yourself that the seeds of loving-kindness are already there, and that they are waiting for you to water them. You don't need to make them grow, blossom, and bear fruit all at once.

If you do feel loving and friendly toward yourself, savor these feelings while allowing them to ebb and flow. Take delight in them without trying to make then stay or become more profound. This provides practice in allowing joyful feelings to simply be present without getting too attached to them. During this experience of love, you may drop the words altogether or simply use the essential sentiments conveyed: "free," "well," "loving," "happy." As the loving feelings wane, you can resume the statements.

It's helpful to treat yourself with kindness no matter what experience you have. It's not uncommon to feel bored with sitting still and repeating the blessings. When this happens, acknowledge the thought that the practice feels boring and bring a little kindness to yourself for feeling bored. Remind yourself that everyone has these kinds of thoughts and feelings, then return to your statements. The key here is that you can foster loving-kindness even in the presence of unpleasant feelings.

Thoughts and feelings of unworthiness, anger, or hatred may emerge. They too are not uncommon and may also be handled with kindness. Experiment with opening to and allowing such feelings. One option is to kindly acknowledge the feelings and thoughts, and then simply return to the statements. Alternatively, you can imbue the experience with loving-kindness by directing the blessings toward yourself for having difficult feelings, or toward the feelings of unworthiness, anger, or hatred, as if the emotions were another person. Yet another option is to envision the part of you that's angry or hateful, and direct the statements toward that specific part of you. Some people imagine a younger part of themselves who has been hurt and needs a soothing voice of kindness. All of these approaches provide an opportunity to gift yourself with love in the midst of difficulty.

Informal Practice: Meeting the Moment as a Friend

At any time, in any situation, you can repeat these phrases, suggested by Sylvia Boorstein: "May I meet this moment fully. May I meet it as a friend" (2011, 126). This can be particularly powerful when you find yourself caught up in approval seeking, whether you've acted to please others or simply noticed the urge to do so.

• *More of Madeline's Story*

Do you remember Madeline, whose painful childhood experiences included abuse, neglect, and the suicide of her mother? Part of her journey toward healing took place during a loving-kindness retreat. Madeline reported to me that she discovered that she had been the "grim reaper," killing all the love that came her way because it simply wasn't good enough. She had been looking for her mother, and no love that came her way could fulfill that desire.

As she sat with what she thought of as a lifetime of mistakes, in which she had rejected potential love again and again, she felt her feelings and simply repeated, *It is what it is*. This opened the door to acceptance. She also realized that the intentions behind all of her actions, even mistakes, were adaptive, and this allowed her to grant herself a measure of forgiveness.

Then she remembered the purpose of the retreat: to water the seeds of loving-kindness. She returned to her statements: "May I be at peace. May I feel love in every cell of my body. May I know my radiant, true nature. May I be happy and truly free." Although she didn't think there actually were seeds of loving-kindness within her, she persisted with her statements.

Then it occurred to her that the only thing she'd ever really desired could be summed up in one statement: "May I find my way home." Never having had the loving home she so desired,

Madeline had fantasized what it would be like to have one. To Madeline, home was the place where she would be loved unconditionally, and where she would be missed if she left, valued, and appreciated—a place where she could take off her mask and just be herself. So Madeline shifted to this new statement and repeated it to herself again and again: *May I find my way home. May I find my way home. May I find my way home.*

As she opened to her desperate desire for coming home, she experienced an elaborate vision. She saw herself in an aspen grove where eventually the trees made a reclining chair for her. She sat in the chair, which swayed in a gentle breeze, and the heavenly, golden aspen leaves fluttered around her. Sitting there, she thought that after a lifetime of insomnia and hypervigilance, she could finally feel safe and sleep peacefully. As she settled in, in every cell in her body she felt that she was home, and she wept tears of relief and gratitude.

This profoundly healing vision was the fruit of Madeline's long-term mindfulness and loving-kindness practice. It had been nourished by her willingness to simply observe her experience and allow her practice to transform her. When she granted herself stillness and silence, Madeline realized that opening to her painful feelings about the abuse, neglect, and being cut off from love actually led to her salvation. Opening to the depth of her desire for home allowed her to find it where she never suspected. After the retreat, she said, "The abstract idea of finding my needs met inside myself, which had never made much sense to me, became a concrete experience. The powerful emotions that arose guaranteed that I would remember this as strongly as any physical experience."

A Loving Hand

While Madeline's experience was profound, subtler experiences can also affirm our inner loveliness. After many years of mindfulness meditation practice, I made loving-kindness toward myself my sole meditation practice for an entire year. It was a lovely journey home to myself. As the year progressed, I was able to be more present and accepting in life. I felt lighter, and my self-criticism was less frequent and less intense. Of course, there were many times when loving-kindness slipped away, but it gradually became easier to access this loving presence of mind and my true nature. I now realize that it's always available, waiting for me like an old friend.

Over the course of that year, I experienced many subtle and wonderful little surprises. Here's a funny example: Sometimes when I feel physically ill, I also feel low emotionally and am more irritable and self-critical. On a really busy day, I got a sore throat and a fever. I came home worried that I might be sick the next day too. When I went to bed, I noticed my hand on the pillow with my thumb tucked into my fist as I rested on my side. The side of my hand looked like a little mouth, just like Johnny, the talking-hand character created by Señor Wences in the 1950s and featured on *The Ed Sullivan Show*. If you're too young to remember this, you can see it on YouTube.

With that unexpected recognition, I smiled. As I continued to look at my hand, Johnny, the little talking hand, seemed to be uttering my spontaneous thoughts: *You'll be okay. It's been a hard day, don't worry.* The voice was kind and sincere, rather than sarcastic and chiding as it might have been in the past. I was able to rest and fall asleep.

Reflection: Creating Personalized Loving-Kindness Statements

As you practice loving-kindness meditation, you may feel that certain words or even entire phrases don't sound quite right for you. It's fine to change them to something that rings true. Just be careful not to change them too frequently, because consistency of the statements helps build the concentration that's so helpful to any meditation. As you create your own blessings, consider what you need in order to contribute more heart and meaning to your life. If you choose to create a loving-kindness statement of your own, come up with something that supports your primary intention to relieve your suffering. As Madeline did, rely more on your heart than your head when creating loving-kindness statements.

Here's an example of how slightly changing your loving-kindness blessings may be beneficial. If strong feelings of unworthiness are an issue for you, you may find it comforting to use phrases such as "May I open to my true, radiant nature" or "May I accept myself exactly as I am."

Here are some other statements to consider. I offer them as examples, not what is right for you. Please feel free to use them or not. You can experiment by saying them to yourself silently and listening to see if they speak to your heart. If not, use your intuition to create phrases that work for you.

- *May I be free from fear.*
- *May I be safe and protected from harm.*
- *May I accept myself exactly as I am.*
- *May I be healthy in mind and body.*
- *May I be free from mental suffering.*
- *May I be free from physical suffering.*
- *May I find balance and ease in life.*
- *May I be filled with loving-kindness.*
- *May I be present and truly free.*
- *May I feel love in every cell of my body.*
- *May I be open and embrace my experience.*
- *May I be at peace.*
- *May my heart be open and free.*

Once you have three to five blessings that fit for you, write them in your journal. You can also record them elsewhere if you wish, perhaps putting them in your smartphone as a note or printing them on a beautiful piece of paper. You'll probably memorize them soon, but in the meanwhile you may wish to keep them available to glance at where you meditate or wherever you need them.

Reflection: Exploring Your Innate Loveliness

Gently settle in with a few minutes of Mindfulness of the Breath. Then take some time to reflect on loving-kindness and your experience with the practices in this chapter. Notice your thoughts, feelings, and bodily sensations. Just let these experiences come to you, simply noticing whatever happens within you. When you're ready, write some of your thoughts and feelings about loving-kindness in your journal.

Informal Practice: Practicing Loving-Kindness During Activities

At any time, say your loving-kindness phrases while performing daily activities. Notice what you experience when you extend loving-kindness toward yourself in day-to-day life.

Summary

Through mindfulness and loving-kindness meditation, we can open to the loveliness that resides within us and take huge strides toward healing the childhood wound that causes chronic people pleasing. With patience and persistence, we extend more love and acceptance toward ourselves and learn that within ourselves we already have what we need. We become less fearful and can dare to let go of trying so hard to please others, freeing us to love and connect authentically and let people see us without the mask of chronic niceness. We also expand our capacity to say no when we need to and lovingly address conflict with others.

8

Befriending Your Emotions

Watch a baby for some time and she'll demonstrate how natural emotions are. For example, when the baby wakes up, she alerts her caregiver with a whimper, then a cry, and then an angry cry, depending upon her circumstances and when her caregiver comes to tend to her. We are all born with emotions, and sometimes simply understanding this can help us judge them less and let go of struggling with them.

Emotions give vibrancy to life and provide vital feedback about what is important to us. Joy comes when we see a baby or hear good news. Anger arises when we feel we've been mistreated. If we didn't have emotions, life would be dull and flat, and we'd be walking around like zombies.

Even though emotions bring a kind of juiciness to life, we understandably react to the wound of feeling unloved and unlovable, along with the resulting chronic people pleasing, by trying to cut off painful emotions. We take the edge off by diverting our attention to things like television, eating, drinking alcohol, or surfing the Web. We may complain about others hurting us instead of focusing on how we feel about it. Often we fight difficult feelings so reflexively that we automatically deny them altogether. While the intention is to protect ourselves, struggling with emotions actually brings more emotional pain.

In this chapter, you'll explore how the lessons of mindfulness—being aware, getting off of autopilot, letting go of judgments and preconceived ideas, letting things be, and seeing things through the eyes of kindness—can help you handle your emotions in a radically different way. Extending these qualities to emotions helps us bestow friendship, openness, and compassion on them.

As we turn toward our emotions with compassion, we take a step toward healing the childhood wound. Opening to our deep desire for love and the vulnerability of wanting to be loved enables us to open to the love that we've been searching for all our lives (Welwood 2006). Holding these and all of our emotions with great compassion sets the stage for creating peace in the midst of turmoil, much like a loving mother soothing and comforting a suffering child, enabling us to act more intentionally and wisely instead of being ruled by emotions.

Befriending Emotions

In the external world, we tend to turn toward our friends and run away from our enemies. Befriending our emotions can help us turn toward the truth of our experience instead of running away from it. It can also help us be with whatever arises, even if what arises is unfriendliness toward our emotions.

Beliefs About Emotions

Exploring what we believe about our emotions and how we relate to them is important in befriending them. In response to the childhood wound, we tend to cut ourselves off from our emotions, perhaps due to a belief that they will hurt too much. In addition, many people are inculcated with the belief that certain emotions are bad, unbearable, or shouldn't be felt, acknowledged, or expressed. "Stop that crying, or I'll give you something to cry about" is a saying that has taught many children to suppress or deny their emotions and teaches the lesson that nothing good can come from attending to emotions. In addition, if children aren't supported when they experience emotions, they develop a sense of aloneness and feel incapable of enduring emotional difficulties. All of these beliefs influence how we relate to our emotions, and all bring the potential for deep psychic suffering.

Good or Bad? Don't Know!

It's difficult to let go of the battle with emotions when we judge them as bad or good. Emotions are really neither bad nor good; they are experiences from which we can learn if we pay open-hearted attention. Here's an old tale that illustrates this point: A wise old Chinese farmer's prized stallion bolted out of the corral. His neighbor said, "Oh, isn't this terrible?" The farmer gently replied, "Maybe, maybe not. Just don't know." When the horse returned with a herd of wild mares, the neighbor said, "Isn't this wonderful?" The farmer said, "Don't really know." When the farmer's son broke his leg while riding one of the wild horses, the neighbor said, "Isn't this terrible?" The farmer kindly replied, "Don't know." Later, when the army didn't enlist the farmer's son because of his broken leg, the neighbor said, "Isn't this great?" The farmer replied, "Maybe, maybe not. Don't know."

As with the farmer, if we stay open and nonjudgmental toward our experiences, including our emotions, we find that we really don't *know* that they're bad, unuseful, overwhelming, or however else we might judge them. And as the farmer did, we might find that staying open and nonjudgmental helps us handle whatever comes our way with greater ease.

Everything Changes

Many of my clients come to me holding the belief that if they open to a strong, difficult emotion, it will never change or end and may even overwhelm or kill them. Knowing that emotions are impermanent can help you befriend them. Through mindfulness practice, you'll gain a deep firsthand experience of the temporary nature of everything, including emotions. This understanding will make it easier to let them come and go without struggling with them, granting you greater ease with emotional pain.

Intentions Toward Emotions

To befriend our emotions, Miriam Greenspan, author of *Healing Through the Dark Emotions: The Wisdom of Grief, Fear, and Despair* (2003), suggests examining our intentions toward them. Most people, including people pleasers, proceed with the intention of banishing difficult emotions. Instead, Greenspan suggests setting an intention to use emotions for the purpose of healing. If we pay attention to our emotions and affirm the wisdom they impart, we can cultivate a kind and accepting attitude toward them.

If you've been suppressing your emotions for years, you may wonder what wisdom can come from the painful emotions associated with chronic people pleasing. Mental health professionals agree that all emotions have positive, adaptive qualities that help us know and tend to our needs. For example, anger tells us that we feel harmed or violated in some way, maybe telling us to right a wrong or stand up for ourselves.

However, emotions can feel confusing. The best way to know what they're telling us is to listen openly. While it may be helpful to know *why* we feel what we feel, this isn't always necessary. In fact, an intellectual examination of our emotions may not serve us well. Sometimes the more we try to figure out our emotions, the more we stay in our heads and in the drama of the moment, causing even more angst. Therefore, the job is simply to be a compassionate witness and open to whatever comes. The process of befriending emotions can help us do just that.

Reflection: Exploring Your Beliefs About Emotions

Gently settle in by practicing Mindfulness of the Breath and Body for a few minutes. Then reflect on your beliefs about emotions. What did you learn about emotions in your early life? Did you learn to believe that they're bad or good? Did you learn that you're bad when you experience or express emotion? What do you think will happen if you let yourself feel emotions? In what ways do you struggle with them? Sit for a while and notice the thoughts that come during this reflection. Take some time to write your thoughts in your journal.

Settle in again by practicing Mindfulness of the Breath for a few moments. Then consider what you'd like to believe about your emotions. Would you like to believe that you don't have to fight them, that you can survive them, or that they can actually be helpful to you? Formulate some intentions toward your emotions—for example, an intention to be open to them and learn from them. How would it feel to adopt an intention to use emotions for healing? Take some time to write about these reflections in your journal.

Acknowledgment of Emotions

An important step in befriending emotions is to consciously acknowledge that they are present. Let's say you feel anxiety about what someone thinks of you. If you aren't consciously aware of this emotion, you're a prisoner of anxiety and automatically react to it. With mindfulness, you can stop, take a breath, and say to yourself, *Anxiety is here*, which can help you step back from the drama of the moment and recognize what's happening. This kind of simple recognition is important in the process of befriending your emotions and grants you more freedom to respond wisely instead of reacting out of old beliefs and feelings. Please be patient with yourself as you work on this. It takes time to develop this type of relationship to emotions, and even with practice, sometimes your emotions will remain below your radar and cause reactivity. That's just part of being human.

Informal Practice: Acknowledging and Labeling Emotions

Throughout the day, check in with yourself by taking a conscious breath and noticing your emotions. If an emotion is present, acknowledge and label it.

For example, simply say to yourself, *Resentment is here* or *Anxiety is here*. In addition, experiment with extending kindness to it by following the advice of Zen master Thich Nhat Hanh and, with fear, for example, saying, "Hello, Fear. How are you today?" (1991, 53).

In my mindfulness classes, I give my students an assignment to do this informal practice for a week. Many students return reporting the same experience: when they acknowledge and label an emotion, it either softens or goes away. Most likely, this is because they have momentarily let go of struggling with it.

However, please understand that the point of this practice isn't to make emotions go away; the point is to relate to them in a more skillful way. If we cultivate a loving acceptance of emotions, part of which is simply recognizing and welcoming them, we can let them move through us and learn from them. Even when we have difficulty doing so, we are still developing greater acceptance of ourselves.

Letting Go of the Struggle with Emotions

When we run from emotions, we add to the feeling of being unacceptable that we felt as children. We abandon ourselves repeatedly and slip further away from our inner loveliness and wisdom (Welwood 2006). Fortunately, we can reverse this damaging cycle by mindfully acknowledging, labeling, and befriending all of our emotions, pleasant and painful.

When a difficult emotion arises, you might tense up and have thoughts such as *This is not okay*, *I can't stand this*, *Just get a grip*, or *Why can't you just be happy?* On the opposite end of the spectrum you might want to hang on to anger so others will finally see that they should appreciate you, thinking, *I'll show him* or *She'll be sorry*. Either way, the struggle adds intensity to an already difficult situation. Mindfulness can help you be aware of this struggle, including your judgments about the emotions and about yourself for having them.

By recognizing and allowing emotions to be present, you don't add more suffering on top of what's already there. Many people say that when difficult emotions arise, they feel anxious or angry toward themselves. Then they try to talk themselves out of the feelings, only to experience more anxiety if they aren't successful in doing so. The drama continues as they analyze and judge the whole process, and ends only when they manage to divert their attention away from the emotion. In the case of chronic people pleasing, we might do that by focusing on others' needs. However, as discussed earlier, this only perpetuates the chronic people-pleasing cycle. In addition, it deprives us of valuable information that our emotions are trying to convey.

As you gradually stop trying to suppress, deny, or empower your emotions, you can develop compassion toward yourself instead of anger or disappointment, even when you're struggling to allow emotions to be present. With this approach, emotions are more likely to come and go, rather than building up or hanging around all day. This allows for greater peace in life and allows you to choose more skillful responses to the situation from which the emotions arose. For example, instead of withdrawing and swallowing resentment, as people pleasers often do, you might be able to open to the emotion and then, as it settles, speak assertively and kindly about a concern.

Meeting painful emotions with awareness and compassion is an active and courageous response especially after years of holding in emotion. It takes a lot of energy to struggle with emotions, so allowing is a wise use of energy. The practice of mindfulness can help you open to and calm your emotions so you can communicate and act more skillfully. However, do keep in mind that befriending emotions is a gradual process that takes patience and practice.

Like most people, you may find that as your mindfulness practice deepens, you become aware of pervasive displeasure and dissatisfaction arising from a constant desire for things to be different than they are. Humans have a tendency to automatically experience the moment as unacceptable. Through mindfulness, you can become aware of moments of unpleasantness and let go of the struggle against them. Often, you're likely to find that the moment is actually fine just the way it is. This awareness can resolve many emotions and bring the possibility of clarity, balance, and joy in the moment.

Similarly, you may judge yourself as unworthy simply out of habit and then evaluate nearly everything as confirmation of your unworthiness. This sets you up for being unable to see and experience the love you so desire when it is actually present, resulting in a sad sense of dissatisfaction with life in general. Mindfulness will help you be present with emotions long enough to see that feelings of unworthiness may simply be a habit, rather than a true reflection of what's happening in the moment or who you really are.

Informal Practice: Grounding Yourself When Overwhelmed with Emotions

When you're feeling overwhelmed by emotion, give yourself a large dose of awareness of present-moment sensations. For example, if you're taking a drink of water, notice the feel of your hand as it touches the water bottle, sense the other hand twisting the cap off, and notice the sensations of bringing the bottle to your mouth. Observe any wandering of the mind and come back to the feel of the bottle touching your lips, the sensation of the water in your mouth, and so on. This can help you ground yourself and possibly open to the difficult emotion and relate to it more skillfully. Remember, this practice is a way to simply feel more grounded when you're experiencing difficult emotions; it isn't intended as a method for getting rid of those emotions.

Reflection: Exploring Unacknowledged Emotions

Because denial and suppression of emotions play a big role in chronic people pleasing, it's important to open to unacknowledged emotions. For several days, notice emotions as they arise during the day and practice acknowledging them. Each evening, reflect on your experience of that day, the emotions that arose, which you tried to get rid of, and which emotions you didn't experience. Then spend some time writing about your unacknowledged emotions in your journal. This may give you an understanding of where your emotional life needs attention. As you continue to practice mindfulness, your emotions may become more evident, giving you a chance to befriend even those emotions you automatically banish from your awareness. (Adapted with permission from Ron Siegel's 2010 book *The Mindfulness Solution*.)

Putting It All Together: RAIN

Mindfulness teacher Michele McDonald created a four-step process that encompasses the approach to emotions outlined above, captured by the acronym RAIN:

R Recognize

A Allow

I Investigate

N Non-identify

R = Recognize

Consciously recognizing that an emotion is present helps you get off of autopilot and out of denial. In his book *The Wise Heart*, Jack Kornfield describes this recognition eloquently: "With recognition our awareness becomes like the dignified host... Recognition moves us from delusion and ignorance toward freedom" (2008, 102). Simple, kind recognition of an emotion can help you free yourself from its tyranny.

A = Allow

Once you recognize an emotion, letting go of any struggle to change or fix it can help you open to what's actually happening. As you notice emotions, experiment with gently telling yourself, *It's okay to feel this, I can handle this*, or *Just allow it in this moment*. In addition, imagine cradling your emotion as if it were a crying baby, as Zen master Thich Nhat Hanh (1991) suggests. Remembering and practicing the attitudes of patience, beginner's mind, nonjudging, and nonstriving, described in chapter 1, can be helpful for allowing emotions. You've had many years of practice in fighting emotions, so when it comes to allowing them, take things slowly, one moment at a time.

You don't have to try to banish resistance if the emotion is more than you can allow in the moment. You don't need to force anything to happen or make anything go away. If allowing feels impossible in the moment, you can compassionately recognize the resistance and allow *it* to be present. Then work with resistance using the RAIN process.

I = *Investigate*

When difficult emotions emerge, we tend to get caught up in a story about the situation. We try to figure things out or justify or get rid of the emotions, or we castigate ourselves for having them. A more fruitful place for the investigation of emotions is in the body. What sensations do you feel in association with the emotion, and where do you feel them? Do you feel heat, heaviness, or contraction? You might gently name the emotion, as well. If exploring anxiety, for example, you could say to yourself, *This is what anxiety feels like*, as you explore the sensations. While exploring the sensations associated with an emotion, experiment with holding them, and yourself, compassionately.

Intense sensations may feel overwhelming, making it quite difficult to observe them. If this is the case, gently place your attention on a part of the body that isn't affected by the emotion, perhaps the toes or the breath. After gathering your attention, go back to exploring the sensations associated with the emotion.

N = *Non-identify*

When suffering, you may feel alone and think of your suffering as unique and personal. Although suffering is a part of everyone's experience, you may feel as though you're the only one in pain.

Many years ago while on a retreat, I experienced what I thought of as extreme bouts of drowsiness and mind wandering, which lasted for days. During one unfocused meditation in which I fell asleep, I opened my eyes to see the room filled with about one hundred other people, and I assumed all were experiencing perfectly blissful meditations. Negative thoughts about myself in relation to everyone else emerged, along with feelings of unworthiness and anger. Of course, others in that room were suffering. When I reminded myself that many people in that room had similar experiences, I felt a sense of belonging and comfort, which I so needed.

When you realize that suffering is part of the human experience, you can take difficulty less personally and open to a comforting sense of belonging. I imagine that you've experienced the relief of knowing another person shares your feelings. As you practice mindfulness with difficult people-pleasing moments, simply reminding yourself of the universal quality of suffering may be soothing.

Exercise: Practice RAIN

You will be most successful in using RAIN in difficult moments if you've practiced it when not stressed. To practice, first settle in with a few minutes of Mindfulness of the Breath. Then experiment with remembering a people-pleasing moment that was emotionally difficult. As best you can, bring it to mind as if it's happening in the moment, recalling it as vividly as possible, with a variety of sensory details. If this elicits an emotion, practice RAIN with it: recognize the emotion, allow it, investigate it, and let go of identifying with it. Remember to be gentle with yourself. Also consider taking some time to write about this experience in your journal.

• *Robert's Story*

Arriving at my office one day, I found a client, Robert, a forty-year-old insurance agent, father, and mindfulness student, waiting for me in the hallway outside the locked door. I greeted him and said I was sorry that he'd had to wait outside in the hallway.

When we started the session, Robert's bravery was evident as he reported that he felt anxious and disconcerted about his wait in the hallway. He wondered if I'd forgotten him or didn't care enough about him to show up. In addition, he'd heard me chatting with someone as I exited the elevator and thought I liked the other person more than him. My heart went out to him as I coached him to notice and befriend his feelings. As he acknowledged them, he sank his attention into his body and witnessed the anxiety morph into shame, then sadness about his past and how it had influenced his feelings, and then kindness toward all of it. This practice helped him to let go of his story and bring comfort to himself.

Informal Practice: Using RAIN as Needed

When you recognize that a difficult emotion has arisen in daily life, acknowledge the emotion and experiment with bringing your attention into the present moment. This alone may ease the emotion. If the emotion continues, practice RAIN for as long as your situation allows, allowing, investigating, and not identifying with the emotion.

Informal Practice: Using RAIN with Specific Emotions

Choose a particular emotion and commit to practicing RAIN with it regularly, perhaps daily, for a week or even a month.

Summary

The practice of mindfulness can help you create a friendly attitude toward your emotions, opening the door to receiving their wisdom and using them to promote healing. Practice patience and nonstriving to open to them with authentic kindness. This will allow them to resolve more quickly than if you fight them.

9

Self-Compassion

In all spiritual traditions, compassion is a prescription for living a connected and blessed life. Compassion includes heartfelt awareness of suffering and the wish to relieve it. For example, the biblical story of the Good Samaritan, who aided an injured traveler, provides a heartwarming example of compassion toward one's fellow human beings. In the Buddhist tradition, compassion is described as the quivering of the heart in response to suffering, and it's what initially set Gautama on the path to enlightenment and becoming the Buddha.

In a dharma talk, Jack Kornfield once said, "When love meets suffering, there is compassion" (2009). This applies equally to compassion toward others and toward yourself.

The Challenge of Self-Compassion

Many people in my classes say outright, "I don't understand how to be compassionate toward myself" or "I don't even like myself; how can I be compassionate toward myself?" Given how the common wound that we all share cuts us off from our innate goodness, these comments make sense. When we don't understand our innate worth and loveliness, we can't offer ourselves compassion. But when we open to our nature of love and are aware of our suffering, self-compassion arises naturally. This allows us to be kind to ourselves in the midst of suffering. By helping us open to the love and sorrows of our lives, mindfulness and loving-kindness meditation forge a path toward self-compassion.

When I get bound up in people-pleasing frustration and worry, compassion can release me from that bondage. Self-compassion helps me to soften into the moment and accept myself just as I am, which is exactly what I was looking for in the first place. In this chapter, I'll help you explore the practice of self-compassion, why it's important, and how you can cultivate kindness toward yourself.

Informal Practice: Setting Self-Compassion Intentions

Create statements of your intention to practice self-compassion, then use them to help you grant yourself this kindness. Here are some suggestions you might work with: "I intend to be kind to myself when I __________." "I intend to be kind and gentle toward myself and my mistakes." "I intend to notice and let go of harshness toward myself." Upon awakening in the morning or at any time, remind yourself of your intention to be kind to yourself as best you can. Doing so, especially in difficult moments, touches your innate desire to be happy and will strengthen your resolve to be compassionate with yourself.

Self-Compassion Helps Others

When we're able to see our own suffering and offer ourselves compassion, we increase our ability to see and relate to the suffering of others. This allows feelings of connection and warmth toward others' suffering to arise more freely. We begin to experience being part of the web of life—the very thing we've sought for so long through approval seeking. In addition, we begin to take our suffering less personally because we see that all beings have similar experiences. Moreover, feelings of connection are no longer dependent upon others; they're available from your own heart at any time. What a relief!

The Three Components of Self-Compassion

Kristen Neff, a leading researcher and teacher in self-compassion, has identified three factors that contribute to self-compassion: mindfulness, self-kindness, and a sense of common humanity (2011). In the sections that follow, we'll explore these factors and how they can help you cultivate self-compassion.

Mindfulness

As discussed, chronic people pleasing often entails perfectionism and feelings of self-criticism and blame. To practice self-compassion during such times, you first need to be aware that you are in such a moment. Mindfulness can help you observe people-pleasing thoughts and feelings and gain some freedom from them, thus giving you many new perspectives, including self-compassion.

Recall my client, Robert, who feared that I didn't care for him. As he waited for me in the hall, he brought his attention to the present moment and noticed his painful thoughts and feelings. Prior to mindfulness training and therapy, he would have denied those thoughts and emotions altogether. Mindfulness allowed him the choice to bestow compassion on himself for feeling afraid and abandoned, instead of swallowing hurt feelings. This, in turn, granted him the opportunity to address his feelings with me and feel more connected with me as a result.

Reflection: Exploring Harshness Toward Yourself

This exercise will help you be aware of a tendency to be harsh with yourself when you're in people-pleasing mode so that you can begin to practice self-compassion instead. Bless yourself with a few minutes of Loving-Kindness Meditation, as described in chapter 7. Then, without trying to analyze things too much, reflect on the questions below (inspired by Neff 2011). Notice thoughts as they come to mind, and record them in your journal:

- *What happens inside when you get caught up in efforts to please someone? Do you judge your actions or yourself harshly to make sure you do the job right? Do you tense up as you strive for perfection? What do you say to yourself? In what ways are you harsh with yourself, if any? Do you ignore your own needs? What do you feel in your body?*
- *What happens inside when you think someone doesn't approve of you or something you've done? What thoughts come? How do you speak to yourself? Do you use a harsh tone of voice with yourself? What does this feel like in your body?*

Self-Kindness

A key element of self-compassion is self-kindness (Neff 2011), the practice of being warm and understanding toward yourself at any time, but for our purposes, especially when you get stuck in habitual people-pleasing mode. As you practice mindfulness, and particularly after the preceding reflection, you may notice how harshly you treat yourself on such occasions. Given that we mimic our parents' criticisms, and that perfectionism and feelings of unworthiness and anger tend to go hand in hand with chronic people pleasing, it isn't surprising that you'd be harsh with yourself. However, harshness only adds to your suffering.

Self-kindness is a way to dissolve this harshness, allowing you to support yourself in the moment. It's a big step toward healing the childhood wound that causes habitual approval seeking, so remember patience and kindness even when you don't feel kind toward yourself.

Understanding the origins of your habitual approval seeking and seeing that it isn't your fault can help you bestow kindness on yourself. For example, an inability to say no stems from needing to please your parents in an effort to receive acceptance as a child. When you bring kind understanding to yourself and your inability to say no, you begin to heal from the original wound. You might say to yourself, *Of course it would be difficult to say no. It's hard to feel this way.* Being kind toward yourself grants you the opportunity to actually feel the warmth of the kind understanding and acceptance you've longed for. In the words of John Welwood, a psychotherapist and pioneer in integrating psychological and spiritual work, "Though you often try to get others to understand you, the understanding that heals the most is your own" (2006, 117). Part of self-kindness is letting go of harshness when you realize you aren't being kind to yourself.

Reflection: Exploring Your Beliefs About Self-Kindness

Gently settle in by practicing Mindfulness of the Breath and Body for a few minutes. Then reflect on your beliefs about self-kindness. As you grew up, how did your primary caregivers handle times when you didn't please them? What happened when you didn't follow their rules or comply with their expectations? Did they use harsh criticism or call you a bad girl or bad boy? Did they withdraw their love or give you the silent treatment? Did you feel unloved, unworthy, or that something was wrong with you? What did you learn that influences how you treat yourself when you aren't catering to others? Take some time to write your thoughts in your journal. Can you see that the origins of your chronic people pleasing aren't your fault? Can you bring kind understanding to yourself? If not, experiment with offering yourself kind understanding for not being able to do so.

It Feels So Odd

Self-kindness may feel impossible if you have a deeply ingrained belief that you're unloved and unlovable. With these beliefs, not only would you not think about being kind to yourself, you'd probably be inclined to think you deserve harshness or abuse instead. In addition, the idea that you must be tough on yourself in order to please others makes self-kindness difficult. You may think that if you let up on this harshness, you'll become a ne'er-do-well.

All of these beliefs generate compulsive negative thoughts and feelings of shame and unworthiness, making it difficult to clearly see interactions and resolve conflicts. Guilt and shame can keep you from taking true responsibility, rather than blame, for actions that may have caused harm. The intentional practice of self-compassion is a potent remedy for all of these problems.

Reflection:
Creating Compassionate Self-Statements

Kristin Neff (2011) recommends speaking compassionately to yourself. This exercise, which is inspired by her approach, will help you formulate statements of self-compassion that you can use when you're treating yourself harshly. Look through the following list and identify which statements would work well for you:

- *Dearest, I am sorry that this is hard for you.*
- *I can say no without having to justify it to others. It isn't my job to take care of everyone all the time.*
- *It's difficult to feel like I don't fit in, but I have the right to be who I am.*
- *It's hard to feel unworthy of love, and I am worthy of it.*
- *Nobody is perfect, including me.*
- *How can I best take care of myself right now?*

In your journal, record the statements that spoke to you, along with any others you might come up with that touch your heart. As with your loving-kindness statements, make your list user-friendly and keep it available for moments when harshness arises. Consider recording the list in your smartphone as a note or printing it out on a beautiful piece of paper.

Informal Practice: Extending Kind Words to Yourself

In everyday life, notice people-pleasing moments. When they occur, speak to yourself kindly, using your self-compassion statements or repeating your loving-kindness statements from chapter 7 a few times. Be open to the feelings that arise.

Loving Touch

At a loving-kindness retreat I attended some years ago, I noticed other retreat attendees holding their hands over their hearts. I tried it myself and found that it was helpful to have a physical sign of kindness and caring while saying my loving-kindness blessings. It helped me actually feel the love and compassion I was cultivating.

In the midst of a chronic people-pleasing moment, you can provide yourself with that same loving touch. Physical affection toward yourself can help you open to physical feelings of self-compassion that you may have stifled for a long time.

Informal Practice: Extending Loving Touch to Yourself

Try it now: Experiment with physical gestures of caring toward yourself. While it may feel uncomfortable at first, tapping into your intention to be kind and then practicing a physical gesture can help you feel the kindness.

Perhaps during a moment of anxiety about what others think of you, you can offer yourself kindness by putting your hand over your heart, hugging yourself, or caressing your face with your hands. Then you could offer yourself some kind words. This may take some practice, but with time you can cherish your own touch. Let go of trying to make yourself feel anything; instead, simply notice whatever feelings arise from this loving touch. Sometimes warm feelings are present, and sometimes they aren't.

Once you've identified gestures of loving touch that feel natural to you, you can use them when you're beset by harsh self-treatment. Be sure to practice this in places where you feel safe and unexposed. Notice any feelings of warmth that arise.

Informal Practice: Approaching Daily Activities with Tenderness

Notice your attitude as you perform daily activities. Do you perform self-care and household chores with a sense of tension or harshness, demanding efficiency and perfection? Do you act harshly toward yourself as you brush your teeth, scrubbing them really hard? Do you walk from place to place pounding your feet on the ground? As you notice, practice kindness and tenderness with yourself and the activity, softening and letting go of tension.

Common Humanity

Given your people-pleasing tendencies, there are probably times when you think you have to earn people's love or feel as though you've failed in attempts to do so. These experiences probably leave you feeling alone and isolated. During such times, you can remember your common humanity by kindly reminding yourself that we all suffer and we all have human frailties, such as making mistakes or being disappointed (Neff 2011).

As mentioned, everyone experienced the childhood wound that can result in the difficult cycle of chronic people pleasing. Perhaps the feelings of being unloved and unlovable, which result in this wounding, are what breed the deep sense of being alone. Through mindfulness, we can open to remembering that this is a common experience, allowing us to take our suffering less personally and feel comforted that others experience this too.

During a meditation class I led for faculty members at a large university hospital, we discussed our common humanity. Then, during a group meditation practice, I looked out at the participants and saw a woman's grimace soften and gradually disappear. After the meditation, she reported that she began the meditation feeling irritated at herself for hurting someone's feelings but then reflected on our common humanity and was comforted to think of all the people who had done similar things and felt the same way.

Since chronic people pleasing includes striving to be perfect, remembering that we all have frailties can help you accept yourself as you are. It takes courage to accept your frailties, especially if perfectionism has been an important way to try to make others love you. With mindfulness you can help accept your humanity and further your journey toward freedom from compulsive approval seeking.

Reflection: Exploring Your Common Humanity

Settle in by practicing Mindfulness of the Breath and Body for a few minutes. Then reflect on the questions below. Notice thoughts as they come to mind, and record them in your journal:

- *Recall a few people-pleasing moments that you remember fairly clearly. Did you feel isolated or alone? Where did you feel that sense of isolation in your body?*

- *What aspects of chronic people pleasing bring the greatest feelings of aloneness and isolation? Do you worry about someone not caring for you? Do you feel forlorn when you don't receive the approval you seek?*

- *How are you reacting to the feelings of aloneness as you recall them now? For a few moments, experiment with acknowledging the feeling of isolation and allowing it to be present. Practice RAIN with the feeling. What happens?*
- *Reflect on the following self-compassion statements, which relate to our common humanity:*
    - *Everyone shares the wounding of the heart that brings about the suffering I feel now.*
    - *Since everyone suffers in this way, maybe I don't need to take this so personally.*
    - *Many people feel that things are their fault. I am not alone.*
    - *No one can please others all the time.*

Summary

Mindfulness, self-kindness, and sensing your common humanity can help you cultivate self-compassion. Your self-compassion will grow as you continue to practice mindfulness and loving-kindness meditation. All of the informal practices in this chapter will also be helpful. Please know that self-compassion is a gradual practice that takes patience and persistence. Sometimes you'll be able to offer yourself compassion, and at other times you'll get caught up in harshness and self-loathing. However, as you continue to remind yourself of your self-compassion intentions and trust in the evolving nature of this practice, you can incline your heart toward self-compassion and practice it more consistently. When you find comfort in your own arms, you give yourself the gift of love that you have sought for so long and ease the fear that fuels the chronic people-pleasing cycle.

10

Living with Intention, Heart, and Meaning

It takes courage to let go of old behaviors and try new ones, especially when the old behaviors are driven by the fear-based beliefs that fuel people pleasing. You can find the bravery you need through mindfulness and loving-kindness practice. Tapping into your heartfelt values and intentions is also helpful. Knowing how you want to be and act in any given moment and committing to living in accordance with these values and intentions will help you choose behaviors that are right for you.

This chapter explores intentions and offers practices and reflections that will help you align your life with your values. This is a key step in freeing yourself from old patterns of behaviors. After years of living according to what others want, you can reclaim your life and follow your own path.

Intention

In earlier chapters, you began the work of creating new intentions for yourself. Now let's take a step back to examine what exactly intentions are and how they can help you change some of your behaviors and live your life with more heart and meaning. Though "intention" has several definitions, for our purposes, intention is how we want to act or be in the present moment. We can fix our attention and volition on intentions in order to act in accordance with what is most precious and resonant in our hearts.

Intentions reflect what you want your life to stand for. Being clear about your intentions can help you live in alignment with your values by directing your moment-to-moment actions wisely. For example, if you have an intention to be present and connected, your awareness of that intention might help you stop and welcome your partner home, instead of scurrying around doing people-pleasing behaviors.

Our deepest intentions are the one place in life where we actually have a say about things. Many things are beyond our control, but remembering and acting in alignment with our values helps us stay on course when storms of reactivity threaten to toss us around. In *Dancing with Life: Buddhist Insights for Finding Meaning and Joy in the Face of Suffering*, Phillip Moffitt says, "Intention is the pivot point that allows you to dance with life" (2008, 229). The practice of mindfulness can help us move and flow with life and respond according to our values instead of reacting impulsively.

Chronic People Pleasing, Intentions, and Meaningful Behaviors

Because the childhood wound and the chronic people-pleasing cycle create disconnection from the self, it's understandable that you might not know or be in touch with your deepest intentions. When you're hyperfocused on what others want, it's nearly impossible to discern what's truly important and meaningful to you, let alone act on it. You can probably recall numerous times when you acted in ways that weren't in alignment with your values in an attempt to be accepted by others.

Whether or not you're connected to your values and intentions, you're always making choices about how to behave in the present moment. Unfortunately, the desire to avoid painful experiences such as anxiety or feelings of worthlessness often takes precedence over acting out of your heart's wisdom and intention (Roemer and Orsillo 2009). For example, you may value honesty and authenticity but, in an effort to avoid anxiety, react by running from conflict, saying yes instead of no, or being overly cheerful. In that case, the reaction to move away from difficult emotions distances you from your values and inner wisdom. It also perpetuates the chronic people-pleasing cycle.

Once again, what started as a way to gain love and acceptance and avoid suffering paradoxically caused a different kind of suffering. As you become increasingly distanced from what is meaningful and valuable in your life, you perpetuate the disconnection from yourself and end up feeling resentful, angry, or depressed. In addition, you don't engage in behaviors that might help you find yourself again, such as self-care, self-compassion, or following what's true in your heart. All of this heightens the tendency to not act from your values and intentions.

When I became a CPA in an attempt to please my father, I wasn't acting according to what was in my heart. I was acting out of fear of being unloved. Later in life, I felt sad, angry, and depressed about not following the path I thought was right for me. Through mindfulness practice and psychotherapy, I found the freedom to follow my heart and change careers. You too can find the freedom to act on what is genuinely most meaningful to you.

Informal Practice: Using Intentions with Habitual People-Pleasing Behaviors

Review the list of your people-pleasing behaviors from chapter 3 and add any others you've thought of since making the list. Then, as you begin each day, choose one behavior to explore. If you feel the urge to do that behavior at any point in your day, stop, take a breath, and ask yourself, *What's important right now?* or *What's my intention in this moment?* Let's say you want to explore the behavior of jumping in to help without really knowing that it's needed, and that you have the intentions of presence and freedom. When you feel the urge to jump in and help, you could stop, take a breath, and remind yourself of your intentions. This can help you allow others the independence to ask for help if they need it.

Balancing Intentions and Goals

Intentions and goals are quite distinct, and knowing how they differ can help you inhabit the moment and live it with meaning. Intentions are about *how* we want to be and act from moment to moment. Goals are specific things we want to achieve or make happen in the future.

Goals often reflect a healthy desire to relieve our suffering. They can help us organize our lives and get things done. Creating and working toward positive goals that are specific, attainable, and grounded in our values and intentions can help us be productive and feel less stress in general.

But if we get caught up in our goals, we typically spend a lot of time in some imagined future that may not even come to pass. This future orientation can result in anxiety and dissatisfaction in the moment because we haven't achieved all of our goals. Moreover, we lose touch with the present moment and our intentions for how we want to be and act in *this* moment. Letting go of attachment to goals by focusing on what's important in the moment can help us rest in the here and now and discern what is called for. We don't have to get rid of our goals, but we do need to find more balance in life by making conscious decisions about what is important in the present moment.

Mindful Intentions

In addition to helping us tune in to our values and intentions, mindfulness fosters awareness, compassion, and openness, which can influence what we value. We begin to treasure moment-to-moment presence and letting go of some of the struggle with life. We begin to gently shift from focusing on others to attending to our inner experience more often. This, combined with glimpses of our inner loveliness and a deeper connection with the body and emotions, helps us value ourselves and our wisdom. This allows us to create intentions and behaviors that are in alignment with our wisdom. Intentions that often emerge through mindfulness practice are to do no harm; to meet life with awareness, love, and compassion; to open to our experience by letting go of aversion and clinging; and to value all experience, even that which is painful.

Reflection: Exploring Your Values and Intentions

This reflection will help you explore what is most important to you and formulate intentions that reflect your deepest values. First, gently settle in with a few minutes of Mindfulness of the Breath and Body. Then, review the following list of values, adapted with permission from the *Nonviolent Communication Companion Workbook* (Leu 2003), and identify the needs or values that speak to your heart. There are countless potential values, but this list is a great starting place:

- **Connection:** *acceptance, affection, appreciation, belonging, closeness, communication, community, companionship, compassion, consistency, contribution, cooperation, empathy, inclusion, intimacy, love, mutuality, nurturing, respect and self-respect, safety, security, stability, support, to know and be known, to see and be seen, to understand and be understood, trust, warmth*
- **Meaning:** *awareness, celebration of life, challenge, clarity, competence, consciousness, contribution, creativity, discovery, effectiveness, efficacy, growth, hope, learning, mourning, participation, purpose, self-expression, stimulation, to matter, understanding*
- **Physical well-being:** *food, movement and exercise, rest and sleep, safety, sexual expression, shelter, touch*
- **Peace:** *beauty, communion, ease, equality, harmony, inspiration, order*

- **Autonomy:** *choice, freedom, independence, space, spontaneity*
- **Honesty:** *authenticity, integrity, presence*
- **Play:** *joy, humor*

Write all that are important to you in your journal. Then reflect for a moment on whether any other values, beyond those listed here, are important to you. Write those in your journal too.

Next, go through all of the values you've listed and prioritize them. Then create intentions for your life based on your list. You might also want to include some of the mindful intentions mentioned above: to do no harm; to meet life with awareness, love, and compassion; to open to your experience by letting go of aversion and clinging; and to value all experience, even that which is painful. For example, if your greatest values are connection and authenticity, your intention statement might be "It is my intention to foster connection with others while being exactly who I am."

Sit quietly for a few minutes and allow yourself to feel the importance of these intentions in your heart. Commit to allowing them to influence your life. As with your lists of loving-kindness and self-compassion statements, keep your list of intentions accessible by putting it in your smartphone or printing it on a beautiful piece of paper.

Informal Practice: Aligning with Your Intentions

At the beginning of the day, look at your list of intentions and let them resonate inside you. Throughout the day, especially during people-pleasing moments, commit to living by them as best you can while also practicing patience and compassion with yourself. Even when you aren't able to align your behaviors with your intentions, you can still learn from your experience, and your new insight into your behaviors will help you choose differently in the future. Reminding yourself daily of your intentions will strengthen them over time.

Informal Practice: Noticing Attachment to Goals

During the day, notice if your attention is on a goal, especially a goal that involves pleasing others. Notice what happens if you get caught up in the goal. Observe whether you get ahead of yourself, leave the moment, or become attached to making things happen in just the "right" way. Acknowledge all of this and, in the present moment, ask yourself, *What's important right now?* Can you let go of the struggle and align with your intention for whatever is right in this moment? Even if you get caught up in the goal again, reminding yourself of an intention will help strengthen it over time, allowing you to act intentionally in the future.

With chronic people pleasing the goal is to obtain approval, and we certainly get caught up in that. When you can come to presence and notice the pull of that goal, stopping to take a breath and approaching the situation mindfully can help you tap into the intentions of honesty and authenticity and possibly step back from falsely agreeing with others simply to make them think well of you.

Choiceless Awareness

In developing mindfulness, we start with practices that have a laser-like focus, such as Mindfulness of the Breath. These directed meditations help us build concentration and steadiness of attention. Over time, the focus expands to include more of our present-moment experience. Eventually, we drop any particular focus of attention and, with the breath as an anchor, watch the flow of our experience, holding it all in kind, independent awareness. This type of meditation is known as choiceless awareness.

The practice of choiceless awareness beckons us to be completely open to whatever experience presents itself: thoughts, feelings, sounds, or sensations. We simply rest in awareness of these experiences, not choosing, fighting, or encouraging anything in particular as the object of awareness. You might think of choiceless awareness as simply being present with yourself. With practice, you can watch experiences come and go much like bubbles that float into your awareness and then drift away or pop.

Mindfulness practice helps us experience that our awareness is separate from the objects of our awareness. It's likened to a flashlight that can shine on a pile of garbage or on a flower. The beam of the flashlight remains unaffected by either the garbage or the flower; it simply illuminates them. Similarly, the light of awareness is unaffected by thoughts, sensations, or feelings. Resting in awareness helps us compassionately witness all of the experiences in our lives, whether joyful or painful.

Practice patience and nonjudgment with this meditation. Because it has no specific focus of attention, it can seem difficult at first. It is wise to practice choiceless awareness for only a few minutes when you're new to it. Over time you can increase the amount of time you spend in choiceless awareness, and it becomes a beautiful and inviting way to practice.

Formal Practice: Choiceless Awareness Meditation

Pause now to practice Choiceless Awareness Meditation for ten to fifteen minutes total. With time, you can extend the duration of this practice. (An audio recording of this meditation is available at www.livingmindfully.org/ntp.html if you'd like to use it for guidance.)

Begin the practice in a dignified, stable, and comfortable sitting position. Practice awareness of your breath or another aspect of your experience, such as sensations or sounds, for several minutes.

When you feel ready, let go of any object of awareness. Allow your awareness to open to all that arises in your experience: sensations, sounds, thoughts, emotions… Simply sit with awareness, awake and conscious of your experience without trying to make anything happen. Experiment with letting go of any expectations or struggle to hold on to or get rid of anything. When you become aware that you are no longer aware in the present moment, you can do one of two things. You can come to the breath for a moment and then expand to choiceless awareness, or you can simply come back to choiceless awareness.

As you end this meditation, gently open your eyes if they're closed and turn your attention to what you see around you. Give yourself some time to move slowly and gently back to the book or whatever is next in your life.

Bringing Your Intentions to Life

Having explored your values and identified and prioritized some intentions, now you can look at how to bring them to life by putting them into action. After years of trying to behave in accordance with others' desires, this may seem like a challenge. However, through mindfulness practice you can find clarity, nonreactivity, and the courage to act on your intentions. Then you can feel less reactive to the anxiety that may arise when you consider new behaviors such as saying no or speaking your mind when you'd normally agree with others.

As you consider putting your intentions into action, realize that you already have experience with this. In fact, you've probably acted on your intentions even when you didn't feel like doing so. Perhaps you'd rather eat a burger and fries, but because you value health, you typically choose lighter fare instead. Perhaps you'd rather go out to eat, but because you value thriftiness, you usually cook at home instead. So you know how to act on intentions based in your values. Of course, doing so can be more difficult when freeing yourself from chronic people pleasing because of the associated fear and the long-term nature of this cycle. Remember that the practice of mindfulness can help you find the freedom to act consciously, rather than reactively.

Let's say your goal is to act with compassionate assertiveness, in keeping with your values of honesty, integrity, and compassion. But when you think of addressing a particular problem with someone, anxiety arises. You may have thoughts such as *I'll just let this slide* or *What's the big deal; this really isn't a big problem*. This wouldn't be uncommon, especially if you're fairly new to being assertive.

At the point when you feel like walking away from addressing the problem, certain mindfulness practices can help you act intentionally—even something as simple as slowing down, taking a breath, and becoming present.

By this point in the book, you've undoubtedly experienced that taking a conscious breath can be like finding a port in the storm of reactivity. It can help you recognize and let go of struggle with thoughts, feelings, and sensations and gain independence from them. Otherwise your thoughts and emotions will almost assuredly govern your actions. With the steadiness you've established, you can befriend your emotions and practice self-compassion, which allows you to remind yourself of your intentions. This is the point in time when you have true choice and can act from the heart.

• *Adriana's Story*

Adriana, a forty-two-year-old middle manager and mindfulness student, was cooking dinner and found herself feeling increasingly irritable. She felt just plain grumpy, seemingly for no particular reason. As she paused to tune in to her thoughts, Adriana realized that worries about what her boss might be thinking of her were whirling around in the back of her mind. She had been trying her best to please him in order to get a promotion, but she thought she had annoyed him that day. Her mind was spinning with thoughts such as *He thinks I'm terrible*, *I won't get the promotion now*, *He's going to fire me*, and *I'm so stupid.* She was on a future-oriented mind trip in which she didn't get the promotion that could bring her more autonomy and gain others' approval. She tried to push it all away but felt increasingly irritable and anxious.

As she noticed her body tense, she came to presence, took a breath, and recognized the grip of anxiety and her old habit of working overly hard to please others. Standing there breathing, she noticed the people-pleasing thoughts and feelings that were so familiar and how they fed on each other. She practiced labeling her thoughts and observing her emotions using the RAIN process: recognize, allow, investigate, and non-identify. In this way, she interrupted her usual cycle of people-pleasing thoughts and concerns. This made it possible for her to purposefully take care of herself and remember her intentions to live in the present and meet her experience with openness and compassion while also being more assertive.

Instead of remaining trapped in the worry and harshness, which usually tended to last all night, she softened to her own kind words: *Oh, dearest, you are suffering. Everyone makes mistakes. How can I best take care of myself right now?* Then, she decided that the next morning, when she could actually do something about her worries, she would talk with her boss, even though she normally avoided any discussion of their professional relationship with him. Having settled herself, she was able to direct her attention to the sensations of chopping carrots and their sweet aroma as they cooked.

When the worry and harshness returned that night, Adriana sometimes got caught up in them, but she often found the courage to reconnect with her deepest intentions to be present in the moment and be compassionate and kind toward herself. This gave her the peace of mind and heart she needed to sleep well and feel composed when speaking with her boss the next morning.

Adriana's anxiety resulted from her fear that her boss no longer appreciated her, and from being focused on the prospect of not achieving her goal. When she became present, she found a port in the storm of her worry, and by checking in with her intentions, she found a rudder to steer her course. She still kept the goal of the promotion, but she let go of attachment to it and chose to live calmly regardless of what happened. Of course, not getting the promotion would be disappointing, but if that did come to pass, she could meet even that disappointment with kind awareness and respond in keeping with her intention to accept herself and treat herself compassionately.

Reflection: Exploring Intentional Behaviors

Psychologists Lizabeth Roemer and Susan Orsillo (2009) suggest exploring how anxiety interferes with intentional behaviors, causing you to avoid them and instead act in ways that aren't in alignment with your values. This reflection will help you do just that.

You may wish to refer to the list of intentions you generated earlier in this chapter and your list of people-pleasing behaviors from chapter 3, so make sure you have both at hand. Gently settle in by practicing Mindfulness of the Breath for a few minutes. Then reflect on the questions below. Notice thoughts as they come to mind, and record them in your journal:

- *How has chronic people pleasing affected your willingness or ability to engage with your intentions and inner wisdom?*
- *What behaviors have you avoided out of fear of being rejected or feeling unloved? What behaviors have you avoided because you felt unworthy or unlovable? What consequences does this avoidance have? How has this affected you?*
- *How have you behaved in an attempt to gain approval or avoid feelings of anxiety? You may wish to refer to your list of chronic people-pleasing behaviors. What are the consequences of these behaviors?*

Now take a few moments to imagine how you might act if you were freer from people pleasing and living more in alignment with your values and intentions:

- *What behaviors would help you take better care of yourself?*
- *What behaviors would help you take care of others without losing yourself in the process?*
- *What activities or behaviors would make your life more joyful and meaningful?*
- *What behaviors would support your mindfulness practice?*

Here are some suggested behaviors you may wish to consider:

- *Taking time each day to practice mindfulness meditation*
- *Stopping from time to time to take a breath, compassionately notice your experience, and inhabit your life fully*

- *Pausing and remembering intentions that can help you determine what is important in the moment*
- *Practicing self-compassion and patience with yourself when you become mired in people pleasing*
- *Noticing the reactive urge to jump in to help, and then pausing to consider your options*
- *Compassionately addressing problems with others*
- *Saying no when you want to or need to*
- *Expressing your opinion even if it differs from that of others*
- *Following through on intentions that reflect your highest values*
- *Acting authentically instead of being "nice" all the time*
- *Practicing self-care every day*
- *Letting go of self-blame every time something goes amiss*
- *Engaging authentically with others*

After reviewing your intentions and your answers to the questions in this reflection, make a list of behaviors you'd like to cultivate in your life.

Working with Intentions and Behaviors

Now that you've clarified your values, prioritized your intentions, and identified behaviors that you wish to cultivate, you're in a much better position to make choices that are in keeping with your values. Of course, it isn't easy to change habits, especially those associated with a lifetime pattern of trying to please others. The following sections offer some tips to help you foster new behaviors and bring mindfulness, intention, and compassion to the process.

Starting Slowly

Start slowly so you won't feel overwhelmed. If you haven't already, give yourself a week or so to slow down a little and simply observe your approval-seeking behaviors without trying to change anything. This may seem like a small step, but simply observing your behavior helps you gain some independence from your experience. It may also help you notice any anxiety that lies beneath your behaviors and spot situations in which you can practice intentional behaviors later.

Because things tend to go more smoothly when we're feeling rested, nourished, and relatively at ease, it's important to take care of yourself. Start trying out your new intentional behaviors when you feel well, rather than when you feel tired or physically or emotionally upset. As you gain experience with a new behavior, you can expand to using it at other times.

Even on a good day, trying to implement your entire list of new intentional behaviors is probably asking too much of yourself. Working with just one behavior at a time can take the pressure off. Choose a behavior that seems relatively easy, experiment with it, and then move on to others.

When cultivating new intentional behaviors, it's skillful to practice in easier situations first and move to more difficult settings over time. For example, telling the grocery store clerk that you've been overcharged may be less emotionally challenging than declining to help a friend you've never said no to.

Practicing Patience and Self-Compassion

At all times, but especially as you begin practicing intentional behaviors, it's important to practice self-compassion and patience. This can help you feel less pressured and more willing to stay present to consider what's important in the moment.

Stopping Before You Act

When you feel the pull of chronic people-pleasing thoughts and feelings, stop to take a breath and slow down. This break in the action allows you some space between the stimulus (people-pleasing thoughts and feelings) and your behavioral response. This pause can help you remember to work skillfully with your emotions, practice self-compassion, and tune in to your intentions. And this will give you more freedom to act on your intentions, rather than on feelings of anxiety that may arise in the moment.

Letting Go of Expectations

With any behavior, especially new ones, notice and let go of any judgments and preconceived ideas you have about the potential result of the behavior. Your expectations can affect whether you actually engage in a behavior and how you engage in it. If, for example, you expect someone to hate you if you stand up for yourself, you may never stand up for yourself, or you may do it only halfway. If, on the other hand, you expect your behavior to instantly change things for the better, you may put too much pressure on yourself and try too hard, or you may be disappointed when the results don't live up to your expectations and therefore give up without giving the new behavior a fair try.

Adopt a "let's see what happens" attitude and try to think of your actions as experiments. Cultivating a sense of exploration and curiosity can help you keep an open mind, minimize resistance, and be more willing to try behaviors that normally bring anxiety. As you continue to experiment with new behaviors, having a sense of exploration and curiosity may make engaging in new behaviors more interesting.

Beginning Again

Although mindfulness can go a long way in helping you practice new behaviors, there will inevitably be times when you get caught up in old, automatic people-pleasing behaviors. Even those who practice mindfulness regularly spend a good deal of time on autopilot, subject to the sway of reactive thoughts and feelings, which tend to lead to habitual behavior. In other words, even with the dedicated practice of mindfulness, there will be many times when you won't stop, won't take a breath, won't connect with your intentions, and won't act intentionally.

For example, say you're at a party and you want the approval of your host and the other guests. This may elicit many people-pleasing thoughts and feelings, and you may find yourself keenly focused on gaining everyone's approval. You might also find yourself jumping in to help without asking. Then, remembering your intentions, you may think something is wrong with you because you weren't able to be authentic with others or ask your host if help was needed. In addition, you may feel frustrated with what you see as slow progress toward freedom from chronic people pleasing. Given this imagined failure, you may become harsh with yourself, thinking, *I just can't seem to get it* or *I'm worthless.* It's important to understand that everyone slips from time to time. Don't take it personally and give up.

The moment when you notice that you haven't acted in alignment with your intentions is a moment of awareness. No matter what intentional behavior you haven't followed through on or how long you've been lost in reactivity, you get to start over again. This is one of the gifts of mindfulness. In each moment, you have an opportunity to tap into your deep intentions to be aware, patient, and self-compassionate and not get further tossed around by the sea of reactivity. You can ask yourself, *How do I want to be in this moment?* And even if you do get lost in more harshness and criticism, you can begin again.

Supporting Intentions with Self-Compassion

Bringing compassion to yourself for old, fear-based, reactive behaviors can help you heal the past hurts that created the pattern of behavior. It can also stave off further barrages of self-criticism and harshness. Self-compassion will be easier if you remember that your chronic people-pleasing behaviors, including self-criticism, represent attempts to care for yourself. Through mindfulness and loving-kindness practice, you can foster the ability to feel deep self-compassion and treat yourself kindly precisely when you act in ways that aren't aligned with your intentions.

As your mindfulness practice strengthens, you can more quickly, frequently, and easily catch the thoughts and feelings that drive people-pleasing behaviors, increasing your ability to act intentionally. In addition, you strengthen your intentions when you connect with them on a consistent basis. Furthermore, staying in tune with the intention to wake up to your life through mindfulness will build a connection between what you learn about mindfulness and actually living mindfully. This will help keep your mindfulness practice vibrant and relevant.

Informal Practice: Acknowledging Yourself

When you follow through with an intentional behavior, stop and take a breath. Acknowledge the courage it took to act from your heart and grant yourself the gift of compassion no matter what results arise from engaging in the new behavior.

Informal Practice: Extending Kindness to Yourself

When you're unable to act according to your intention or when you act in ways that are counter to your intentions, stop, take a breath, and notice your internal experience. Experiment with letting go of any judgment and offering yourself kindness and compassion instead.

Summary

Mindfulness can help you open to yourself and know what is most important to you in life. With this clarity, you can identify your deepest values and intentions and use them as a guide for how you want to be or act in the moment. Then you can utilize moment-to-moment awareness to find opportunities to reconnect with your intentions throughout the day and align your behaviors with them. When you connect with your intentions, you give yourself the freedom to choose how you act, rather than reacting to fear-based thoughts and remaining enmeshed in chronic people pleasing. By acting based on your intentions, you place yourself firmly in charge of directing your life, opening the door to a life lived more joyfully and meaningfully.

11

Mindfulness with Relationship Difficulties and Conflict

Let's revisit Chris, who had an epiphany in the garden that helped her find a measure of freedom. With ongoing mindfulness practice, she learned to smile at her thoughts and developed the vision and strength to pursue her own path while also creating a more loving, balanced relationship with her husband, Charles. This new path had its challenges, and mindfulness helped Chris stay more grounded in the moment along that journey. Because these changes were also challenging to her marriage, Chris and Charles needed to learn to communicate more skillfully. In this chapter, we'll follow parts of that journey.

This chapter, which focuses on mindfulness with difficulties in relationships and conflict resolution, explores how seeing others and ourselves through new eyes can support happier relationships and minimize conflict. It also brings together several mindfulness practices into a unified approach that's helpful during any difficult interaction, especially conflict. The focus on partner relationships will continue in this chapter. However, you can use these approaches in any relationship.

In a marriage or other partner relationship, you and your partner can practice meditation and the strategies offered in this chapter together. In a loving way, invite your partner to practice with you, while also letting go of trying to push or cajole your partner to do so. Even if your partner chooses not to practice mindfulness, your own individual work can create a ripple effect that can transform those you're close to, including your partner (Psaris and Lyons 2000).

Intention in Relationships

In chronic people pleasing, the unconscious motivations in relationships are often to be nice and compliant and not rock the boat. Therefore, it will be important to tap into the intentions you created in chapter 10. As you practice mindfulness and some of the fear-driven motivations ease, you can more easily connect with intentions of being present, open, connected, compassionately assertive, or balanced in your relationships.

Reflection:
Exploring Intentions in Relationships

Gently settle in with a few minutes of Mindfulness of the Breath and Body. Then reflect on your deepest values in regard to relationships. You might revisit the reflection Exploring Your Values and Intentions, from chapter 10. Think about the difficulties you've experienced in meaningful relationships and how your behavior may have played a role in those difficulties. Be sure to extend kindness and compassion to yourself as you do so. Also, remember that both parties play a role in all relationship difficulties. The point of this reflection isn't to heap blame on yourself or dwell on past difficulties; rather, it is to envision how you'd like to be and behave, moment to moment, in your relationships. Take some time to write your intentions for your relationships in your journal.

Informal Practice: Remembering Your Intentions in Your Relationships

In everyday life, when you come into contact with a loved one, stop, take a breath, and remember your intentions for how you want to be in each passing moment. Then, try to behave in alignment with those intentions. Even if you aren't successful in the moment, you'll learn from your experience, and your new insight into your behaviors will help you choose differently in the future.

Let's say that you're feeling upset with your partner for not letting you know he was going to be late. The intentions of assertiveness and honesty may help you compassionately address the grievance and resolve the situation. However, your ability to be assertive and honest will vary from moment to moment and day to day. If you pay attention over time, you can learn how to act assertively and honestly more often.

The Gift of Seeing Through New Eyes

Just like Chris, who noticed her thought that her husband was silently criticizing her, you can benefit from tuning in to your perceptions of your partner and the effects of those perceptions on the relationship. Mindfulness grants you a kind, conscious, independent perspective—a lens through which you can see your harmful perceptions of yourself and your partner. From this perspective, you can work with those perceptions more skillfully. Seeing yourself and others through fresh eyes can be essential in creating more loving relationships, handling conflict, and navigating changing relationship dynamics.

One painful effect of people-pleasing perceptions is that they create a sense of separateness from others. Chris's thought that there was something innately wrong with her and that she must please Charles at all times kept her from feeling connected to him. In addition, those thoughts created resentment and fueled her deep sense of aloneness.

Jack Kornfield describes this sense of separateness well. Our ideas of who we are arise and solidify like "ice floating on water" (2008, 65). The ice seems to be separate from the water, yet it is made of that very water. Our views of ourselves harden like ice and rob us of feeling our connections. Through mindful awareness, these perceptions will gradually melt, becoming more fluid and allowing us to become aware that we are part of something larger than ourselves. With this sense of belonging we realize we already have the connection that we've been seeking, so we feel freer to address grievances with others and say no when needed.

Just as ice thaws slowly after a long, cold winter, our perceptions also take time to melt after years of reinforcement. Patience, nonstriving, and commitment to mindfulness practice will help see you through those times when your perceptions seem frozen and impossible to change.

Seeing Ourselves Through New Eyes

As discussed, the childhood wound can produce thoughts and feelings that lead to deep and enduring emotional detachment. For Chris, this sense of disconnection grew as she donned the mask of niceness and strove for perfection, which diminished her chances of connecting with Charles in an authentic way. In addition, her fear that she was doomed if she spoke up and that she was to blame for nearly everything kept her from addressing conflict. As a result, she missed opportunities for increased intimacy through compassionate conflict resolution.

Through mindfulness practice, Chris began to melt these frozen, restricted views of herself. She gradually developed a more flexible sense of herself and realized that her self-image and the stories she told herself were mere perceptions and didn't encompass her authentic self. With time, she felt more freedom to accept herself as she was and flow more easily with life.

As she began to feel less fearful, she found that she was able to act in new ways. She often dropped the mask of chronic niceness and let others see her not as eternally agreeable and seemingly perfect, but as a genuine and flawed but beautiful human being. She could turn toward love instead of running from intimacy and conflict. She spent less time worrying about what she thought others wanted from her and trying to do it, and therefore felt less pressured and resentful. All of this helped her be less defensive and more authentically connected, assertive, and willing to resolve conflicts in her relationships. What a relief for Chris and her loved ones.

Seeing Others Through New Eyes

As Chris began to accept herself as a vulnerable and flawed but beautiful person, she started seeing others in the same way. She gradually let go of the expectation that Charles could or should love her perfectly and gave him more space to be exactly as he was. She opened to compassion for Charles and stopped trying to control him with efforts to earn his approval through her perfectionism. With patience and persistence, you can do this too. As Terry Hershey (2011), author, inspirational speaker, and minister, said on his website, "Change happens when we quit clamoring for perfection from imperfect people."

When you see others through new eyes, you unlock the gilded cage, freeing them from living up to the impossible task of making you perfectly happy to repay you for your caretaking. Anger and resentment can recede for both of you once you're freed from unrealistic expectations. This sense of freedom can help people change in other ways, as well.

Another way of seeing others more lovingly is to distinguish people from their behaviors. In addition, recognizing the deep, loving intention to be happy and free that informs their behaviors can change your perspective, even when you feel hurt by others. You can begin to allow them to make mistakes and hold them in compassion even when their behaviors are unskillful and hurtful. This can allow you to soften when conflict arises and speak with a more compassionate voice.

As Chris's practice deepened, she began to see that Charles too was born with innate loveliness and mindfulness. Charles was human and suffered. He too had childhood wounds, perhaps similar to Chris's. He too had a monkey mind. This helped Chris see Charles through the eyes of kindness and soften her judgments during moments of conflict and hurt. If you bring this perspective to your partner, both of you, as well as your relationship, will blossom in profound ways.

Others Seeing Us Through New Eyes

Whether your partner practices mindfulness or not, your practice will help your partner see you as you are. As Chris began to accept herself and let go of her perfectionism and chronic niceness, Charles was able to see her as she genuinely was—as a beautiful and flawed human being. This opened the door to new depth in the relationship as Charles came to know Chris, accept her exactly as she was, and connect with her more authentically.

Seeing the Relationship Through New Eyes

As you notice and let go of some of your perceptions about your relationships, you can gradually let go of the idea that you must constantly attend to others and provide what you believe they need. Again, even if your partner doesn't practice mindfulness, he or she will undoubtedly feel the effects of your practice. This can help both of you gradually let go of some of the unproductive behaviors in your relationship. Perhaps you'll feel freer to seek balance in the relationship and let go of some of your fear-based caretaking behaviors. This, in turn, will give your partner the space to let go of a sense of entitlement. Your relationship can become more balanced, with the relationship contract becoming more equal, loving, and connected. In addition, what was once an unspoken contract can become a conscious, spoken agreement. A bit later in this chapter, I'll outline a peace treaty process that can help forge this kind of agreement.

Informal Practice:
Seeing Your Partner Through New Eyes

When you see your loved one, notice the thoughts that arise. What story are you making up about your partner? Are you imagining what your partner is thinking about you? Do you imagine your partner being ready to criticize you? Consciously acknowledge these thoughts.

Next, imagine that you're seeing your partner for the first time—as you did with the raisins or other food in the mindful eating practice in chapter 1. Notice what happens when you look at your partner in this way. You may become more aware of your perceptions, allowing you to open to the idea that there is more to your partner than you think. This can help you see your partner more kindly and be less reactive.

Dealing with Difficulties

As Chris embarked on her journey toward awareness and freedom after a lifetime of fleeing from even the possibility of conflict, she and Charles faced some challenges in communicating about the changes in their relationship. Chris gradually stopped some of her excessive caretaking behaviors and started expressing her needs and desires more often. For the most part, Charles was relieved to be spared the pressure of her caretaking and proud of Chris for speaking up for herself. However, sometimes he felt understandable confusion or anger as he adjusted to Chris not catering to him and always agreeing with him. The following sections offer some tips on how to deal with the difficulties that may arise as you mindfully redefine your relationship.

Peace Treaties

In his book *Teachings on Love* (1998), portions of which have been adapted here with permission, Vietnamese Buddhist monk Thich Nhat

Hanh outlines a type of peace treaty that can be immensely helpful in any relationship. The treaty involves both parties making a conscious agreement about how to handle grievances before they arise, transforming reactive feelings and behaviors, such as anger, defensiveness, criticism, and harmful comments, into loving speech. In addition to resolving differences, this practice can help both parties feel closer afterward.

The peace treaty invites you to commit to bringing up grievances in a loving way. Both parties agree to refrain from causing further difficulty when either is feeling hurt or angry but also agree to not suppress their emotions. In addition, they agree that before either addresses a grievance openly, they will both practice mindfulness of emotions, opening the door to speaking about the hurt with love and compassion.

This step of turning inward to care for our emotions is very important. As John Welwood writes, "What lies at the core of all grievance is a deep pain and grief about loss of connection" (2006, 76). Practicing RAIN (recognize, allow, investigate, and non-identify) with our emotions can help us befriend those feelings instead of reacting with behaviors that may lead to more rejection and lack of acceptance. Providing comfort and support to ourselves makes it possible to act with integrity and kindness in resolving the difficulty.

The next step in the peace treaty is that the offended partner agrees to ask for a time to discuss the difficulty when both can do so with kind hearts. Both partners agree to respect all feelings and the need for time to process them. The offending party also agrees to reflect mindfully upon how her behaviors might have caused suffering. Upon reflection and realization of the role her unskillfulness played in the upset, the offending partner apologizes.

Note that even if your partner doesn't agree to sign a peace treaty, you can commit to this approach and grace your relationship by observing its principles.

When Chris and Charles created a peace treaty, they found that bringing consciousness to what had been an unspoken, unconscious relationship contract was immensely helpful in navigating the challenges of their changing relationship. This allowed them to broaden their discussion to the concerns each had about how Chris's changes might affect the relationship. Together, they decided to set a specific time to discuss the issue so they could minimize distractions and hopefully speak with more intentionality, love, and respect.

Learning to STAND TALL

When engaging in discussions about conflict, whether in the context of a peace treaty or otherwise, you may find the acronym STAND TALL helpful:

S Stop

T Take a breath

A Allow

N Notice

D Discern

T Turn toward love

A Affirm

L Listen deeply

L Lovingly speak

As you can see, STAND TALL encompasses many aspects of mindfulness that are important in handling relationships with love, compassion, acceptance, and assertiveness. Practicing STAND TALL isn't a linear process; rather, it involves flowing among various aspects of mindfulness. As with the peace treaty, you can practice most aspects of STAND TALL regardless of whether your partner does. It can be applied either before or during discussions, or both.

Let's take a look at how this approach helped Chris before and during discussions with Charles about their changing relationship.

S = Stop

Chris felt the tug of anxiety and unworthiness before and during the discussion. When she did, she stopped and contacted the moment. This helped her notice that she'd been on autopilot. Stopping helps create a pause between the stimulus and automatic reaction.

T = Take a Breath

Taking a conscious breath helped Chris find some calm and a solid place to stand in the midst of her thoughts and feelings. The breath is a vehicle for grounding awareness in the moment and the body.

A = Allow

Allowing and noticing (the next step) go hand in hand. In moments when people-pleasing habits get in the way or you wish to address a grievance, an allowing stance can help you simply settle into the moment. Letting go of the struggle and becoming less reactive is often like being thrown into a pool; after you stop flailing and splashing around, you may find that you can actually stand up in the water.

As Chris slowed down by stopping and taking a breath, she realized that she was awash with thoughts and emotions—so many and in such flux that it was difficult to acknowledge them, much less separate them out. Remembering that her emotions had valuable information to convey to her, she tried to open to them and allow them to simply be. Although she couldn't initially let go of her struggle to suppress or deny her painful emotions, she practiced allowing not being able to allow. Extending this acceptance to herself helped further quell her defensiveness and reactivity so she could open to her experience.

N = Notice

Paying openhearted, moment-to-moment attention helps you gain an independent perspective on what would otherwise be a jumble of stimuli to which you might simply react. When attending to your internal experience, you have sensations, thoughts, and emotions to notice. When you add a conversation, you have the other person's words, body language, and facial expressions to notice, as well as your felt sense of connection (Siegel 2010). This can seem like a lot to attend to mindfully. Patience and continued practice will be helpful.

With habitual people pleasing, you may tend to be vigilant in regard to others' experience and ignore your own. Taking time prior to difficult conversations, as suggested in the peace treaty, can encourage an inner focus. Experiment with noticing and perhaps labeling all aspects of your experience, especially your physical sensations and feelings, from which you may have been cut off for a long time. Noticing, allowing, and bringing compassion to your experience exactly as it is can help you listen and speak calmly and lovingly.

As Chris prepared for the discussion with Charles, she noticed that in one moment she felt dead set on getting Charles to agree that she should quit her job and go back to school. Then, in the next moment, she wanted to abandon the idea. She also noticed that she felt anxious and defensive about what Charles might say. Would he become angry and shout at her? Would he think she was selfish?

Chris noticed that her experience included both grasping (for Charles's approval and agreement) and aversion (to the reactions she feared from Charles and the challenges of discussing these matters). Consciously acknowledging these aspects of her experience and allowing them helped her see her thoughts and feelings simply as events in the mind, granting her further freedom from reactivity. She felt calmer and more able to trust in the process and cultivate a "let's see what happens" attitude. During her conversation with Charles, she could remind herself of these realizations, which might help her continue to cultivate an open attitude.

While in actual conversation, attending to your partner's communication is essential. The first four aspects of STAND TALL—stop, take a breath, allow, and notice—will help you be more present and open to the conversation.

D = Discern

As you notice and relax into the moment, reflecting upon your experience can help you discern, deeply and compassionately, your reactive assumptions, how they are impacting your relationship, and what course of action you might take. Since it isn't the external event but how you relate to it that causes suffering, turning your attention inward for a while is essential.

As you turn inward, consider the following questions (adapted with permission from Fralich 2007) and simply observe what comes to you, including bodily sensations, thoughts, and feelings. You need not go through all of these questions in the moment, especially during a conversation. Choose those that feel most relevant to your situation:

- *What people-pleasing beliefs and other assumptions and feelings am I reacting to now?*
- *How are my assumptions and feelings contributing to the difficulty?*
- *Can I see myself through new eyes?*
- *What stories am I telling myself about my partner and what assumptions am I making?*
- *How are these assumptions affecting the way I work with this situation?*
- *Is my partner intending to hurt me or be disrespectful, and even if this is the case, can I be patient and understanding of my partner's struggle?*
- *Can I see my partner through new eyes?*

As Chris let some of these questions steep inside her prior to the conversation, she realized that she was reacting to childhood memories of her needs not being respected or met and old beliefs that she was unworthy and unlovable. She also understood that her drive to please Charles arose from a desire to gain love and acceptance. In addition, she noticed how her perceptions of Charles fueled her anxiety about the upcoming conversation.

In his book *Nonviolent Communication* (2003), psychologist and mediator Marshall Rosenberg underscores the importance of recognizing the underlying, unmet needs that contribute to grievances and difficult communication. Chris realized that the strength of her desire to get her way arose from having done so much for Charles throughout the years. Her unmet desire to be loved and cherished unconditionally had piled up, and she wanted something in return for everything she'd done.

Be sure to ask yourself if your relationship difficulties are related to unmet needs. In addition, ask yourself if you can tend to your needs in some way. Also consider whether you can help your partner meet his needs as well. Chris attended to her own needs by remembering her true nature and offering herself loving-kindness, then did the same for Charles. She explored seeing herself and Charles through the eyes of kindness and compassion.

During this time of discernment, you can explore possible choices for handling the grievance and meeting your needs. Remembering your intentions for how you want to be in the moment can help you skillfully choose your behavior even in the midst of conflict. While in touch with your values, ask yourself how you might deliberately and lovingly handle the situation. Is there a creative response that you can use instead of your reflexive reaction?

As Chris saw the origins of her needs and reminded herself of her own goodness and Charles's goodness, she decided that an open and compassionate attitude would help her accept the outcome of her conversation with Charles, whatever it might be.

T = Turn Toward Love

Your mindfulness and loving-kindness practice can help you turn toward yourself, your experience, and others with love. When you gain a more independent perspective, lovingly accept yourself, and align with your intentions, you feel more connected to others and less dependent on them for approval. As discussed, this helps you take the risk of being seen exactly as you are, while also helping you see others as unique and lovable humans. It allows you to find the courage to stay present and choose a loving, compassionate course of speech and action.

Even if your feelings are hurt, you can step into your partner's shoes and empathize with her. In addition, discerning your partner's adaptive intentions and separating her behaviors from her common humanity will help you feel compassion. What a gift to feel connected with your partner as a fellow human being and speak about the grievance with love instead of rancor.

We open to giving and receiving more authentic love, perhaps even unconditional love, by opening to our deep desire for it and the vulnerability that accompanies that desire (Welwood 2006). As Chris observed her thoughts and feelings, practiced letting go, and extended compassion to herself, she began the gradual process of opening to these profound feelings, allowing her to more easily turn toward Charles with love and compassion.

A = Affirm

When one partner is a people pleaser, relationships tend to be lopsided. The other partner often holds more power and is in charge most of the time. This imbalance can make it challenging to deal with conflict. It will be important to step back and affirm what you've learned through mindfulness. Acknowledging your true nature, your inner beauty, and your imperfection and common humanity will put you on a more even footing with your partner. You can cultivate a sense of worthiness and belonging that can strengthen you in expressing your opinions and asking for what you want, even if you feel vulnerable in doing so. Experiment with offering yourself loving-kindness and compassion either before or during a difficult conversation. This will help you soothe yourself; it will also help you extend loving-kindness and compassion to your partner and listen more wholeheartedly.

Affirming and attending to your emotions can help you acknowledge and be with the vulnerability associated with asking directly for what you need and want. In his book *Perfect Love, Imperfect Relationships* (2006), John Welwood says that most of the time we simply complain about not getting what we want instead of asking for it directly. He goes on to explain that the complaining and chiding are defenses against being seen, known, and maybe not getting what we want. It's much easier to focus on how others don't give us what we want than to expose ourselves in this way. However, opening to this vulnerability is an important part of connecting deeply.

While Chris was attending to her thoughts prior to her conversation with Charles, she noticed a great deal of internal complaining and defensiveness, with thoughts such as *Charles doesn't care about what I want. He always just does what he wants.* She also realized that a key reason why Charles rarely honored her desires was because she rarely communicated them.

When Chris thought about talking with Charles about this pattern in their relationship and directly asking him for what she wanted, she noticed fearful and vulnerable thoughts: *What if he laughs as me? He'll think I'm selfish.* She stopped, took a breath, and allowed these emotions to simply move through her. In that moment, tears of tenderness flowed and she felt compassion toward Charles and herself. She realized that if Charles could listen to and honor her needs, she'd feel loved, and that for this to happen, she must express her desires. Chris decided to muster the courage to tell Charles that she wanted to quit her job and go back to school.

In a similar way, you can cultivate the presence and nonreactivity that are essential if you are to live in accordance with your deepest intentions. At any time during a conflict, you can affirm what is important by reminding yourself of your intentions. This can help you consciously direct your behaviors even during a conflict. Once you affirm your inner loveliness and the validity of your needs, emotions, and intentions, be sure to acknowledge your partner in the same way. Affirm your partner's sovereignty and your intention to treat both yourself and your partner with dignity and compassion.

L = Listen Deeply

After spending time fostering her clarity and composure, Chris was ready to listen to Charles wholeheartedly. She felt connected with him as she listened to his concerns about the loss of her income if she were to quit her job. She stayed present to his words, body language, and facial expressions, and as she allowed Charles's words to touch her, she attended to her internal experience as well and felt compassion and empathy arising within her. In the moments when she felt like avoiding the subject, swallowing her desire, and submitting to Charles's preferences, she reminded herself to stay present, simply listen, and foster an attitude of "let's see what happens." To listen most deeply and effectively, Ron Siegel (2010), professor of psychology and internationally renowned mindfulness instructor, recommends attending to your partner's experience, your own experience, and the sense of connection between you.

L = Lovingly Speak

Because Chris had listened to Charles deeply and intentionally, she was able to let him know that she heard him, understood his concerns, and empathized with him. An effective way to accomplish this is outlined in Harville Hendrix's *Keeping the Love You Find* (1992), portions of which have been adapted here with permission: mirror (or paraphrase), validate, empathize, and sum up. While this way of communicating takes extra time and effort, it facilitates understanding, connection, and empathy. To give you an idea of how to implement this approach, let's take a look at how Chris incorporated these four elements in her response to Charles.

After stopping to take a breath, Chris mirrored what Charles had said: "If I heard you correctly, while you support the idea of me going back to school to develop a new career, you think we'll have financial trouble if I don't work for a while. You also indicated that you feel a little resentful now and will feel burdened by being the sole breadwinner if I go back to school. Did I understand you?" Charles nodded his agreement.

Next Chris validated Charles's experience, saying, "When I look at this from your perspective, it makes sense that you think we'd be strapped for cash." Although Chris understood why Charles would think this way, she didn't agree that they would have financial difficulties and thought that they simply wouldn't be able to save as much in the short term. Even so, she felt inclined to give in to Charles's wishes and give up her own. She stopped, took a breath, and silently acknowledged her thoughts and feelings. Then she reminded herself of her intention to honor her needs and speak assertively yet compassionately.

With this reminder, Chris felt she could hold herself compassionately while also empathizing with Charles. She had found that she could empathize and said, "I can understand how you would feel resentful and burdened by my desire to quit my job." Charles sighed and, with a look of relief, said, "Yeah, thanks for noticing."

Chris then summed up by combining mirroring, validating, and empathizing. She said, "I hear that you support me in going back to school and that you think we will be financially burdened if I do. I can understand how you would think that and then feel resentful." She could see Charles's shoulders loosen and his general demeanor relax as he said, "You got it." Chris felt a rush of warmth, connection, and relief.

Thanks to this successful communication, Chris felt more confident about continuing to tell Charles her thoughts and desires in a loving and assertive way. Throughout the conversation, before she began to speak she stopped, took a breath, and practiced a condensed version of STAND TALL. In this way, she summoned the courage to turn the conversation to the general pattern of their relationship, in which she submitted to whatever Charles wanted, and the role he might be playing in that dynamic.

An overarching guideline for speaking lovingly is to follow the golden rule: speak to others as you would like to be spoken to. This implies having the intention to do no harm and to speak the truth in a kind way. My friend and colleague Steve Flowers (2009) suggests placing an emphasis on kindness and points out that it may be more compassionate to say what is kind than what is 100 percent true.

Since Chris had the habit of not speaking up, she wanted to be specific and assertive in her speech. She used the following format for assertive speech, which her therapist had explained to her, and which many communications experts suggest. These guidelines helped Chris take responsibility for her feelings and avoid blaming and judgmental speech.

1. When you [briefly describe a behavior],
2. I feel [an emotion]
3. because [briefly explain your way of perceiving this behavior].
4. What I want is [describe it briefly and specifically].
5. Will you [a very concrete, specific request]?

Here's how Chris used this formula for assertiveness in the conversation with Charles: "When you don't ask me what I want and simply go for what you want, I feel resentful and left out. I think you don't care about me and what I want. What I want is to know that you care about me and my desires. Will you ask me specifically what I think and want in regard to issues that affect both of us?"

Charles was silent for a moment. Then he came over to Chris and gave her a big hug. He told her he hadn't realized how hard it had been for her to speak her mind, and then he lovingly agreed to ask her specifically for her input.

Summary

By practicing the skills encompassed by STAND TALL, you can be more present, open, and loving in interactions. This approach can help you find the courage to communicate compassionately and assertively. As you gradually develop self-acceptance and open to the love already within you, your partner's love can become a source of happiness, rather than seeming inadequate. All of these factors will foster a felt sense of connection with both your partner and yourself, allowing you to actually show up for the relationship. The result will be fewer grievances, a more joyful partnership, and an enhanced ability to handle conflict when it does arise. The way Chris practiced STAND TALL was unique to her. As you experiment and use your intuition to discern what's right for you in the moment, you'll find your own ways of using this approach. I hope STAND TALL is a gift that you can give yourself.

12

The Path Ahead

Many people I speak with about mindfulness have a gut reaction, a profound knowing, that this practice is for them. Maybe you've had a similar experience and feel that mindfulness is a good fit for you. Reflect on how you've felt while reading this book and doing the practices and exercises. Does what you've learned ring true for you? If so, you'll probably want to build a regular mindfulness practice.

Having an ongoing practice will help you foster the openhearted awareness and nonreactivity you'll need to continue to apply mindfulness to people-pleasing habits. Without an ongoing practice, you may slip back into simply reacting to the thoughts and feelings that arise during stressful times. Therefore, this chapter explores how to make mindfulness a regular part of your life.

Intentions, Goals, and Commitment

While mindfulness practice can be deeply meaningful and beneficial, weaving it into the fabric of your life can be challenging. As you learned in your work in chapter 10, committing to your intentions and remembering to follow through on them allows you to align your actions with what's truly important to you in life. The intentions to be aware, compassionate, allowing, and kind can help you navigate the joys and sorrows of life, and remembering these intentions can help you choose to practice even when you feel that many other demands infringe on your time. Let your intentions be your guide.

Having a goal is important too. What are your goals in regard to practicing mindfulness? Maybe you have a goal of meditating daily. Perhaps you want to find a mindfulness class in your area or go on a retreat. Maybe you have a goal of reading and working with other books on mindfulness. Having goals for your practice will help you stay on track. Just remember to let go of attachment to any particular outcome. Instead, simply live according to your intentions and allow the rest to unfold.

In our culture, most people's lives tend to be very busy. Given that you're prone to habitual people pleasing, your plate may be overly full. Maintaining a regular mindfulness practice may feel like a daunting challenge. Making a strong commitment to wake up to your life, including your tendency to seek approval, can help you find the patience and persistence to continue and deepen your practice. Consider starting with a commitment to practice five days per week for two months to immerse yourself in the practice and see if mindfulness is for you. If it is, you can make a long-term commitment after the two-month trial period. (I've provided a two-month meditation schedule a bit later in this chapter, in case you need some help in creating a structured practice.) Whatever commitment you decide to make, view it as a gift to yourself, a sign of honoring yourself after years of dismissing or ignoring your needs.

Lots of people think of commitment and discipline as being onerous or punishing, like the Nike slogan "Just do it." I say "just do it with compassion"; that way the process becomes imbued with kindness.

Reflection: Exploring Your commitment to Practice

Gently settle in with a few minutes of Mindfulness of the Breath and Body. Then reflect on your experiences with mindfulness as you worked with this book and how you'd like to integrate an ongoing practice into your life. Take some time to write about this in your journal, then distill your thoughts into a single concise statement, such as "I commit to waking up to my life and finding freedom through establishing a vibrant, long-term practice of mindfulness." As with the intentions you've created while working with this book, record it on your smartphone, a beautiful piece of paper, or an index card. You might want to make several copies. Then post your commitment in one or more places where you'll see it often.

Ongoing Formal Practice

I encourage you to practice mindfulness meditation at least five days per week. Some people dive in and start with forty-five minutes of practice each day, a schedule recommended in most mindfulness-based stress reduction classes. Others prefer to enter the water slowly, starting with shorter meditations and lengthening their practice over time. Notice any judgment about either of these alternatives and let go of it. With either approach, you'll be spending time befriending your mind, body, and emotions and disengaging from automatic responses, and this will help you wake up to a life imbued with wisdom and meaning.

Please consider adopting the following two-month schedule to establish a strong foundation upon which you can cultivate a long-term practice. The meditations build on each other, so I recommend practicing them in the sequence indicated. Patience, persistence, and all of the attitudes of mindfulness discussed in chapter 1 will help support you to practice often, and also when you miss a day of practice.

Give all of the meditations a chance to grow on you. Most people have preferences, but make sure you don't assume that certain practices aren't for you because you didn't take to them from the start. Come to each practice session with beginner's mind; rather than assuming that you don't like a given practice or that it doesn't work for you. Even though I offer a detailed practice schedule below, make the practice your own. Follow your intuition and let go of expectations about how your practice should be structured.

Week 1: Practice the Body Scan for fifteen to forty-five minutes.

Week 2: Practice the Body Scan and ten to fifteen minutes of Mindfulness of the Breath.

Week 3: Alternate between the Body Scan, Mindful Stretching, and Walking Meditation for twenty to forty-five minutes. Practice twenty minutes of Mindfulness of the Breath.

Week 4: Alternate between the Body Scan, Mindful Stretching, and Walking Meditation for twenty to forty-five minutes. Practice twenty minutes of Mindfulness of the Breath and Body.

Weeks 5 and 6: Alternate Mindfulness of Sounds and Thoughts for fifteen to thirty minutes with either the Body Scan or Mindful Stretching for fifteen to forty-five minutes.

Week 7: Practice the meditation of your choice for at least forty-five minutes. If you're using guided audio recordings, experiment with not using the recordings.

Week 8 and beyond: If you had been using guided audio recordings, feel free to resume using them if you wish. Use your intuition to choose the practices that are appropriate for you.

Commitment to continuing to deepen your practice can help you make mindfulness a lifetime practice and a way of life. You may need to challenge your ideas about time and what's worth spending time on. We often think we should be *doing* something with our time, but with experience, you might find that meditation (which may feel like doing nothing) can imbue your other activities with a sense of peace and ease. By taking this time away from doing, you may become even more productive. So on a really busy or difficult day when you feel pressured for time, finding even just a few minutes to meditate can be profoundly beneficial. For example, you might practice between meetings or while waiting in the car to pick up children.

If meditation is to become part of your life, you have to make space and time for it. Setting a specific time of day to meditate will help ensure that you actually get around to practicing. Many long-term practitioners meditate first thing in the morning, which helps set the tone for the day. They do something to wake up, like feed their pets or splash cool water on their faces, and then meditate. I recommend experimenting with meditating first thing in the morning, but if it's not for you, others times are fine. If your life is such that it's difficult to practice at the same time every day, make appointments with yourself at times that work, and then treat them with the same respect you would any other appointment.

Find a specific place to practice in your home. It can be as simple as a corner of a room, but hopefully it will be a location where you won't be interrupted. Make it a welcoming space by adorning it with whatever makes you feel comfortable. Ask family members to be supportive during your practice time by minimizing interruptions and noise. While having a separate space at home is helpful, you can meditate anywhere: on an airplane, in the waiting room at a doctor's office, or on a park bench.

Ongoing Informal Practice

Hopefully you've been experimenting with all of the informal practices in this book. To help build your informal practice, return to chapter 1 and focus on the practices of Stopping to Take a Breath, Eating Mindfully, Being Mindful During Daily Activities, Using Cues for Mindfulness, and Using Your Smartphone Smartly. These practices foster mindfulness of the breath and awareness of simple daily experiences to help ground you in the moment. Through these practices you can more often have a direct, sensate experience of your life, rather than thinking about what you're doing or getting lost in the past or future. This allows you to inhabit your life and experience each moment for what it is: the moment in which you live your life. It allows you to more fully live the only moment you have: the present moment.

As you simply stop, breathe, notice the moment, and allow your experience to be exactly as it is, this ongoing informal practice will help you spend increasingly less and less time on autopilot. I can't overemphasize the importance of letting go of striving with this practice. If you try to use mindfulness to get rid of some feeling or experience or to attain a goal, you'll only add to your suffering.

Also remember that the kind of presence fostered by mindfulness opens the door to living less reactively and with more compassion and insight. From these seeds, the ability to make skillful and loving choices arises. In his book *Dancing with Life: Buddhist Insights for Finding Meaning and Joy in the Face of Suffering*, Phillip Moffitt says, "As I have urged repeatedly…just show up for your deepest intentions, as best you can, and then allow the…truth of awakened presence to do the work" (2008, 167).

Please know that there are many ways to practice informally. The informal practices in this book offer just a glimpse of the endless possibilities. In addition, I hope you'll take some time to work with the approach embodied in the STAND TALL acronym until it becomes second nature. It weaves many practices together, and you can use all or part of it, depending upon the situation. Furthermore, keep in mind the attitudes of mindfulness outlined in chapter 1: patience, beginner's mind, nonjudging, nonstriving, and allowing. All are worth cultivating and will help deepen your practice, both formal and informal. The practices and stories in this book aren't rules for how to pay attention; rather, they are suggestions for working skillfully with your experience. Listen to your heart as you decide how to practice and let your practice unfold as it will.

Informal practice with less complicated, everyday experiences helps you develop the ability to be present during more difficult moments, such as when the urge to engage in people pleasing arises. If you've ever played a musical instrument or a sport, you know that you must start with the basics. For example, if you play the piano, you probably began with scales and simple songs, which prepared you to play more complicated pieces.

Practicing mindfulness with stressful people-pleasing moments can be more difficult than paying attention to the sensations of smoothing the sheets as you make the bed. Having said this, you may find that even making the bed is infused with a worried, approval-seeking quality. You may become aware of physical sensations such as clenched muscles, thoughts like *Oh geez, he'll think I'm not doing a good job* or *I wish he'd make the bed sometimes*, or feelings of shame, irritation, or resentment.

To practice with this example, start where you are: come into mindful presence and simply breathe and notice what's up. Experiment with acknowledging whatever you're experiencing in the moment, and then gently and kindly let go of judgment and shift your attention to the feel of the sheets as you smooth them over the mattress. Sometimes switching your attention in this way can ground you in the moment and put the people-pleasing difficulty into perspective. If, as is typical, your attention returns to the disturbing thoughts, sensations, or emotions, experiment with returning to the sensations of making the bed a few more times.

If the people-pleasing cycle continues to crowd in, explore other aspects of your experience. Staying grounded in the breath, explore, allow, and bring compassion to the direct experience of sensations in the body, as described in chapter 5, particularly those that are probably connected to the emotions at hand. This can be especially important if you've been cut off from your body and emotions for a long time. Feeling into sensations will help you tap into the body's wisdom, creativity, and intuition, which can provide excellent guidance. You might also experiment with labeling the sensations and noticing their ever-changing nature.

In addition, observing and labeling your thoughts, as described in chapter 6, can help you find some peace with them. One of the more useful informal practices for me is Noticing Your People-Pleasing Focus, from chapter 6. You might also soothe your emotions by befriending them with the RAIN practice, as described in chapter 8.

It can be powerful to notice and let go of harshness with yourself by blessing yourself with loving-kindness, as described in chapter 7, and self-compassion, as described in chapter 9. These approaches will help you remember your true nature, including your inner loveliness and common humanity. Practicing any appropriate aspects of STAND TALL, as described in chapter 11, will also be helpful. Any of these practices can help you tap into your intentions for how you want to be in the moment, as described in chapter 10. Your intentions are key in helping you respond to the moment in a way that's aligned with your values. No matter which practices you use at any given time, trust the simple practice of awareness and your intuition, and remain connected to your intention to wake up to your life. With this approach, you'll find your way from moment to moment.

Having worked your way through this book, you've become familiar with many practices that can help you free yourself from habitual people-pleasing thoughts, emotions, and behaviors. To move forward, focus on those that have been most helpful, or choose whatever seems most appropriate in the moment. If you need more structure, choose one thought, emotion, or behavior and work with it for a week or two, then switch to another. If you go this route, you may want to begin with emotions, thoughts, or behaviors that aren't highly charged so you can build your confidence for expanding your practice. Alternatively, you may wish to begin by targeting an emotion, thought, or behavior that tends to create a lot of problems in your day-to-day life. With either of these approaches, you might find it helpful to consult your lists of chronic people-pleasing thoughts, feelings, and behaviors, from chapter 3, then decide which aspects of habitual people pleasing to work on.

Perfectionism and Practice

The tendencies that influence your life will also influence your mindfulness practice. If, like most people prone to chronic people pleasing, you tend toward perfectionism, you may hold yourself to impossible standards in your mindfulness practice. You may think that you should be able to practice without becoming distracted, or you may believe that your practice should grant you the ability to say no immediately whenever appropriate. You won't practice mindfulness perfectly. That's impossible. Remember that the benefits of mindfulness sometimes come suddenly and other times filter in gradually. Knowing this can help you allow your practice to be as it is in the moment and trust in its unfolding. I encourage you to let your practice evolve naturally without trying to force things.

Realizing that perfectionism has the adaptive aim of earning love and acceptance and that perfectionism isn't your fault will help you cultivate kind understanding of this coping strategy and compassion toward it. Notice your inner experience when perfectionism arises, and let your kind understanding allow you to extend compassion to yourself. Also remind yourself of your inner loveliness and your fallible humanity, and continue to foster this awareness through loving-kindness meditation and ongoing self-compassion.

Forgetting and Remembering

In formal or informal practice, an experience of awakening occurs in the very moment that you discover you haven't been paying attention in the moment. View it as a wonderful opportunity, imbued with the freedom to begin again. Even if you've felt lost, asleep to your experience, or caught up in habitual approval seeking for hours, days, months, or years, you can always start over again. This is one of the great gifts of mindfulness. When you notice that you haven't been present, that you've lost track of your practice, there you are, present in the moment and ready to begin again.

Summary

As you practice, please remember that mindfulness is simply noticing the present moment with an open, allowing heart again and again and again, without trying to make anything happen. Through mindfulness, calm nonreactivity and insight arise, allowing you to be more emotionally resilient and increasingly free from the anxiety associated with the need to please. In this way, you gain the ability to choose balanced and compassionate behaviors that are in alignment with what is deeply important to you.

As you open to your innate loveliness and that of the world, you become less reliant upon others for proof of your worth and better able to follow the path that is meaningful to you. Your love can blossom and spread to your dear ones and to all beings, and you can open to their love too. Through this opening, you can give love unconditionally to yourself and your loved ones, and through your awakened heart and mind, you can heal the childhood wound and gain freedom from the painful and ultimately ineffective cycle of people pleasing.

I send you heartfelt wishes for freedom and love as you cultivate your mindfulness practice.

May you be at peace.

May you accept yourself exactly as you are.

May you know your inner loveliness.

May you be happy and truly free.

Resources

You don't have to go it alone with mindfulness. Learning from and practicing with others can help deepen your practice. Here are a few resources that will help you connect with mindfulness instructors and groups.

Mindfulness-Based Stress Reduction Classes (MBSR)

To find an eight-week MBSR class, contact these organizations:

- Mindful Living: www.livingmindfully.org. MBSR classes in Houston, Texas, and individual mindfulness training via Skype.
- The Center for Mindfulness in Medicine, Health Care and Scietyat the University of Massachusetts Medical Center: www.umassmed.edu/cfm. Many mindfulness resources, including a worldwide MBSR program finder.

- Mindful Living Programs: www.mindfullivingprograms.com. Live, online, real-time classes.

Meditation Groups and Retreats

Here are a couple of resources for information on meditation groups and retreats:

- Mindful Living: www.livingmindfully.org. Retreats and meditation groups.
- Inquiring Mind: www.inquiringmind.com. Journal with a website that provides a listing of mindfulness meditation groups and retreats in the United States. (Note that this site uses the terms "insight" and "vipassana" for mindfulness.)

Finding a Therapist Specializing in Mindfulness

Several forms of therapy emphasize mindfulness. The websites of the professional organizations listed below include search engines for locating practitioners who specialize in these forms of therapy:

- Acceptance and commitment therapy (ACT): www.contextualpsychology.org/act. Individual therapy used for a variety of concerns.
- Mindfulness-based cognitive therapy (MBCT): www.mbct.com. A treatment for depression relapse prevention, usually offered in a group class format.
- Dialectical behavior therapy (DBT): www.behavioraltech.org. A form of therapy that combines individual and group sessions and is highly effective for people who are easily overwhelmed by their emotions.

References

Boorstein, S. 2008. *Happiness Is an Inside Job: Practicing for a Joyful Life.* New York: Ballantine Books.

Boorstein, S. 2011. *Solid Ground: Buddhist Wisdom for Difficult Times.* Berkeley, CA: Parallax Press.

Brach, T. 2011. *Unconditional Love for the Life Within.* (Dharma talk, Insight Meditation Community of Washington, Washington, DC, October).

Braiker, H. 2001. *The Disease to Please: Curing the People-Pleasing Syndrome.* New York: McGraw-Hill.

Carter, L. 2007. *When Pleasing You Is Killing Me: A Workbook.* Nashville, TN: B&H Publishing Group.

Einstein, A. 2011. *Essays in Science.* New York: Open Road Integrated Media.

Flowers, S. 2009. *The Mindful Path Through Shyness: How Mindfulness and Compassion Can Help Free You from Social Anxiety, Fear, and Avoidance.* Oakland, CA: New Harbinger Publications.

Fralich, T. 2007. *Cultivating Lasting Happiness: A 7-Step Guide to Mindfulness.* Eau Claire, WI: Premier Publishing.

Greenspan, M. 2003. *Healing Through the Dark Emotions: The Wisdom of Grief, Fear, and Despair.* Boston, MA: Shambhala Publications.

Hendrix, H. 1992. *Keeping the Love You Find.* New York: Pocket Books.

Hershey, T. 2011. "Unfair" (Sabbath Moment 197). http://archive.constantcontact.com/fs009/1100948702336/archive/1107807984781.html (accessed September 26, 2011).

Kabat-Zinn, J. 1990. *Full Catastrophe Living: Using the Wisdom of Your Body and Mind to Face Stress, Pain, and Illness.* New York: Bantam Dell.

Kabat-Zinn, M., and J. Kabat-Zinn. 1997. *Everyday Blessings: The Inner Work of Mindful Parenting.* New York: Hyperion.

Killingsworth, M., and D. Gilbert. 2010. "A Wandering Mind Is an Unhappy Mind." *Science Magazine*, November, p. 932.

Kornfield, J. 2008. *The Wise Heart: A Guide to the Universal Teachings of Buddhist Psychology.* New York: Bantam Books.

Kornfield, J. 2009. *Why and How We Become Enlightened.* (Dharma talk, Spirit Rock Meditation Center, Woodacre, CA, October).

Leu, L. 2003. *Nonviolent Communication Companion Workbook: A Practical Guide for Individual, Group, or Classroom Study.* Encinitas, CA: PuddleDancer Press.

Moffitt, P. 2008. *Dancing with Life: Buddhist Insights for Finding Meaning and Joy in the Face of Suffering.* New York: Rodale Books.

Neff, K. 2011. *Self-Compassion: Stop Beating Yourself Up and Leave Insecurity Behind.* New York: HarperCollins.

Nhat Hanh, T. 1991. *Peace Is Every Step: The Path of Mindfulness in Everyday Life.* New York: Bantam.

Nhat Hanh, T. 1998. *Teachings on Love.* Berkeley, CA: Parallax Press.

Orsillo, S. M., and L. Roemer. 2011. *The Mindful Way Through Anxiety: Break Free from Chronic Worry and Reclaim Your Life.* New York: Guilford Press.

Psaris, J., and M. Lyons. 2000. *Undefended Love.* Oakland, CA: New Harbinger Publications.

Rapson, J., and C. English. 2006. *Anxious to Please: 7 Revolutionary Practices for the Chronically Nice.* Naperville, IL: Sourcebooks.

Roemer, L., and S. M. Orsillo. 2009. *Mindfulness- and Acceptance-Based Behavioral Therapies in Practice.* New York: Guilford Press.

Rosenberg, M. 2003. *Nonviolent Communication: A Language of Life.* Encinitas, CA: PuddleDancer Press

Rushdie, S. 2012. *Joseph Anton: A Memoir.* New York: Random House.

Salzberg, S. 1995. *Lovingkindness: The Revolutionary Art of Happiness.* Boston, MA: Shambhala Publications.

Selye, H. 1956. *The Stress of Life.* New York: McGraw-Hill.

Siegel, R. 2010. *The Mindfulness Solution: Everyday Practices for Everyday Problems.* New York: Guilford Press.

Welwood, J. 2006. *Perfect Love, Imperfect Relationships: Healing the Wound of the Heart.* Boston, MA: Trumpeter Books.

Williams, M., J. Teasdale, Z. Segal, and J. Kabat-Zinn. 2007. *The Mindful Way Through Depression: Freeing Yourself from Chronic Unhappiness.* New York: Guilford Press.

Micki Fine, MEd, LPC, is the founder of Mindful Living in Houston, TX and a certified mindfulness teacher. She was awarded this credential from the University of Massachusetts Medical Center, where Jon Kabat-Zinn founded the renowned Center for Mindfulness. She holds a master's degree in counseling psychology and is licensed as a professional counselor. She has been in private psychotherapy practice since 1990, and currently teaches mindfulness in her private practice, The Jung Center, and Rice University. To find out more about Fine, visit livingmindfully.org.

Foreword writer **Diana Winston** is coauthor of *Fully Present*. Heralded by the *Los Angeles Times* as one of the nation's best-known mindfulness teachers, she has been teaching since 1993 in a variety of settings, including hospitals, universities, corporations, non-profits, and schools.

FROM OUR PUBLISHER—

As the publisher at New Harbinger and a clinical psychologist since 1978, I know that emotional problems are best helped with evidence-based therapies. These are the treatments derived from scientific research (randomized controlled trials) that show what works. Whether these treatments are delivered by trained clinicians or found in a self-help book, they are designed to provide you with proven strategies to overcome your problem.

Therapies that aren't evidence-based—whether offered by clinicians or in books—are much less likely to help. In fact, therapies that aren't guided by science may not help you at all. That's why this New Harbinger book is based on scientific evidence that the treatment can relieve emotional pain.

This is important: if this book isn't enough, and you need the help of a skilled therapist, use the following resource to find a clinician trained in the evidence-based protocols appropriate for your problem.

Real help is available for the problems you have been struggling with. The skills you can learn from evidence-based therapies will change your life.

Matthew McKay, PhD
Publisher, New Harbinger Publications

If you need a therapist, the following organization can help you find a therapist trained in cognitive behavioral therapy (CBT).

The Association for Behavioral & Cognitive Therapies (ABCT) Find-a-Therapist service offers a list of therapists schooled in CBT techniques. Therapists listed are licensed professionals who have met the membership requirements of ABCT and who have chosen to appear in the directory.

Please visit www.abct.org and click on *Find a Therapist*.